World Healing World Peace

Poetry

I0155698

2014

Volume II

inner child press, ltd.

<u>Credits</u>

Compilation

Janet P. Caldwell

Foreword

Fahredin Shehu

Preface

William S. Peters, Sr.

a few Words

Dr. hülya n. yilmaz
Dr. Peter C. Rogers

Cover Graphics

Chyna Blue
edifyin' graphix

General Information

World Healing ~ World Peace Volume II
Inner Child Press, ltd.

1st Edition : 2014

Publisher Information
1st Edition : Inner Child Press :
intouch@innerchildpress.com
www.innerchildpress.com

ISBN-13 : 978-0615996103 (Inner Child Press, Ltd.)

ISBN-10 : 0615996108

$ 16.95

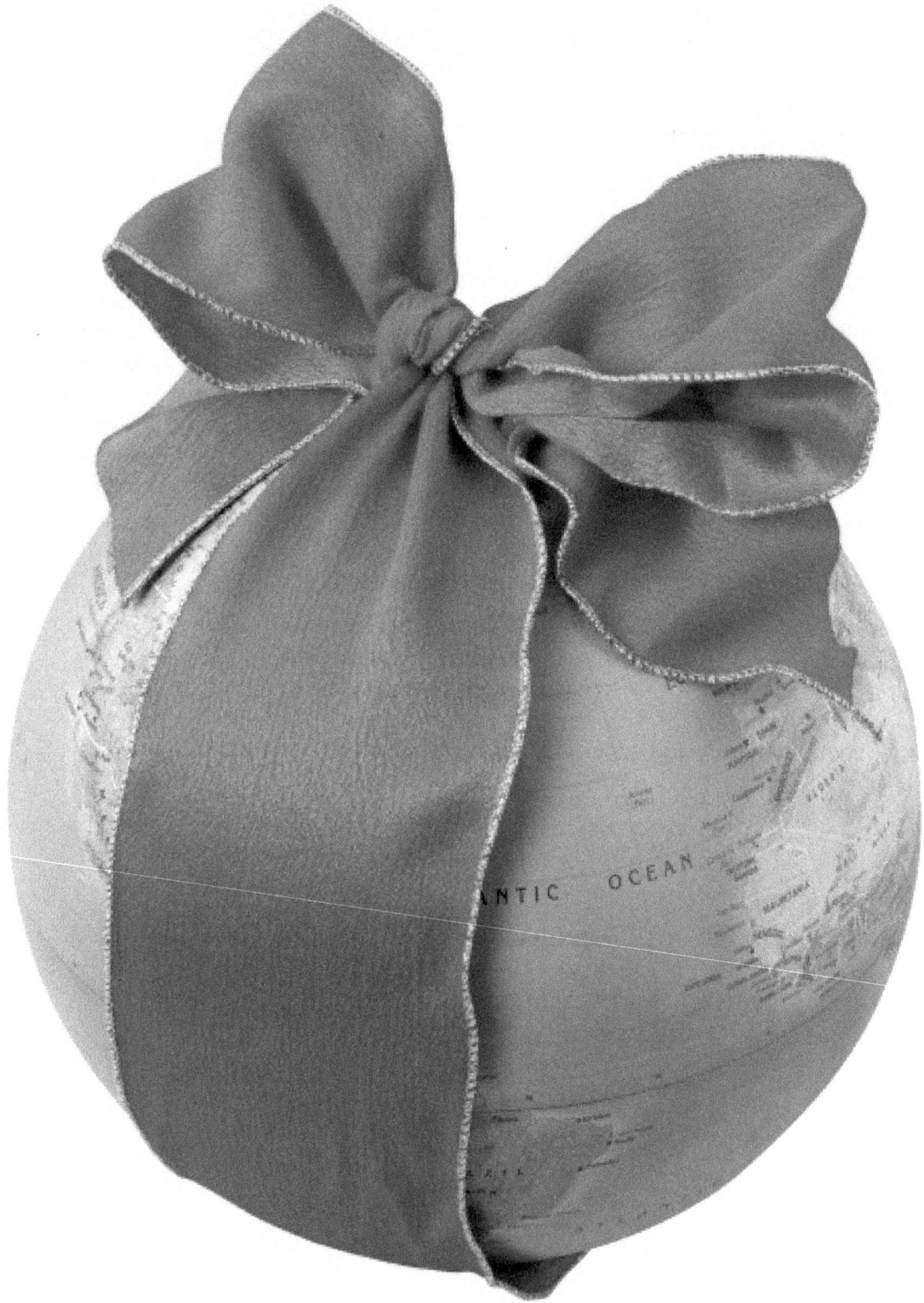

Dedication

This offering is dedicated to Humanity

. . . and it's resurrection.

my Sun is Orange

my morning Sun is orange
The yellow is stained
with the Blood of my People
for that is what we
are reminded of
each day

when it rises from the East
to greet the world
i see my world
clearly

we once lived with a hope
that the atrocities of Hate
War
and indifference
would go away
but it did not

my hope has been misplaced
somewhere
and i can not remember
where i have set it down

it might have been that day
i lost my arm
or that day
when my Father was jailed
or that day
when my Sister was killed
she was only 3

no, i think i lost my hope
the day
my Mother no longer cried

her eyes have been dry
for many a year now
and somehow
by some grace
she still has enough love in her

to hug me
once in a while
through that pained smile
that still adorns her face
just so she won't completely break

there is a noise i hear
it is a loud silence
that stays with me
through my callousness
for the gunfire
and the bombs
and the screams
i can not hear them

they have long ago
assaulted and killed
the dreams of my Family
my village
my people
and it is now working on
Humanity

where is the sanity
in this methodology
to be found

every day is "Ground Zero"
where i live
every where i look
i see Ground Zeros
and we have lost count
of those who
are no more
because of what you call War

but you and i
never had a dispute
that i know of
If so, please tell me what i did wrong
to cause you harm
that you should exact such wretchedness
upon me
and others like me

i know not of the Politics
of it all.
i have never met a Politician
are they so different
than we the people ?

if it's Oil
i give it to you
if it's right
take it freely
i will not raise nor put my hand
against that
of my Father's children

there was a time
when all i thought of
was simply
finding Joy in my life
i have since given up that quest
for i see far too much
of that other stuff
which deserves not a name

my Sun is no longer Yellow
but i do pray my Brother
that yours is

my Sun is Orange

This is dedicated to all the Villages, Peoples across our Globe who must endure the
Politics and Sickness of War.

© 1 July 2013 : william s. peters, sr.

Foreword

to the Members of One Body

"Human beings are all members of one body. They are created from the same essence. When one member is in pain, The others cannot rest. If you do not care about the pain of others, You do not deserve to be called a human being."

Mosleh al-Din Saadi Shirazi
13th century Persian poet, from Shiraz

~ * ~

There are myriads of words Men had had uttered throughout its historical life journey leaving the rich legacy of conscience, endeavor, struggle to remain the essence of Unique and Uniqueness of Creation. The Word has killed Men and the Word is able to cure Men. The Word has burned many hearts and many evil hearts has burned the Word in Men's History. Today as in every age again there are some people unable to remain passive bystanders for the wounds of the world.

This world as it was cursed by us, Men alone, to suffer in continuation of her existence. At least what they may do is screaming to tell the Truth, and the Truth is that the World today needs the Healing.

We have to always be amazed with the power of some individuals to bring together those very Human who scream to say the Truth, the Truth of their Capacity, the Truth of their Creativity, the Truth of their Justice and the Truth of their Human Potentials in an "Understandable Language", that goes beyond simplicity, people who are set alone, themselves alone, to create a beautiful Word as manner of healing themselves, healing others and the World, who are scarifying their time, their creativity and their entire being.

This Anthology typically represents the Beauty created with sacrifice...the palette of colors and the nuances, sounds and the grandeur of pain, the hollow voices that comes from eternity going through the prism of nowadays turbulences, walking from country to country from continent to another to gather in one spot, in one aim as an arrow to hit the target of contemporary Men's consciousness.

The reader of these lines shall be delighted to read the elements of the others' beings the quintessence of these incredible Poets and Poetesses, without wanting to distinguish names since for me there is no the best Poets, there is always the best time and the best mood to have the splendor and joy in absorbing ones word, when the one is in tune with the being, with the breath, and with the momentum. They do as they want to say to us: "We have tamed our wildness, come and join us, come and rejoice, for Peace shall belong to all it is a right not a privilege."

I'm indeed much honored to be the one who writes the open Word for this Anthology and express the gratitude to William S. Peters, Sr. who made it possible for me possible to be among these incredible words created by these incredible Humans, and my gratitude reaches the whiteness of the clouds. Only those who are able to build bridges among nations, religious background, ethnicities and genders; are able to understand the importance of this Noble effort. This is indeed a noble endeavor!!!

Thank you Inner Child Press

Fahredin Shehu

March, 2014
Prishtina Kosovo

Fahredin Shehu

Born in Rahovec, South East of Kosova, in 1972. graduated at Prishtina University, Oriental Studies.

Actively works on Calligraphy discovering new mediums and techniques for this specific for of plastic art.

Certified expert in Andragogy/ Capacity Building, Training delivery, Coaching and Mentoring, Facilitating etc.

In last ten years he operated as Independent Scientific Researcher in the field of World Spiritual Heritage and Sacral Esthetics.

Preface

It is not just because i have children and i have concerns for their safety and welfare, but the fact of the matter is you may have children too. Actually we are all children of this wonder filled Creation who inhabit this Awe Inspiring Planet we call Earth.

When i think in terms of World Healing ~ World Peace, like most of us there is much about us that needs our attention, adjustment and resolution. I like most of us could sit and complain the remainder of our lives away about all that is wrong. The predominant aspect of what i would like to ultimately transfer in the way of energy to every on i can, is that we have the ability to effectuate the changes we desire. We have the power to reconcile our existence to that of our Dreams of Utopia. "Our World" is inherently one of abundance and i believe there is enough for all of us to coexist in a peaceful, loving manner. For too long we have allowed the few to control the many. This would include most of our institutions from Religion, Politics, Education, Business, Food, Medicine, Media and Finance.

Our desires for "Things" along with the rampant Greed we witness has gone just about as far as we should allow. However, in order to make the much needed equitable adjustments for parity, we must first examine and correct the archaic consciousness' we hold to unwittingly. The depth of our indoctrination fed to us by the controlling class is a tangled web filled with deceits and ulterior motives and agendas that do not serve the masses of people who have need for such basic things as Drinking Water, Food, Medical Attention and the lack of War and Strife.

Many may ask, "How can we achieve this end?" . . . well, i have always been told that "every journey begins with the first step". Many have already taken that initial step, while some are waiting for the right motivation.

We have chosen the medium of Poetry and Prose to relay our messages from around the world. In this our second effort to evoke a higher level of participatory consciousness we hope that you find the words that moves you to care enough to be moved to a certifiable action that contributes to the good of us all.

Our aspiration here with this effort of World Healing ~ World Peace Poetry 2014, is not only to just produce a book, but to distribute the book and get it into the hands of our World's Policymakers. We have a campaign to deliver copies to every member Country of the United Nations as well as every voting member of The United States Congress. we can not do this alone. There is a Fund Raising Campaig still active to achieve this goal. If you can not contribute, please do take the time to share the message!

Funding Campaign
http://www.gofundme.com/3gvqks

The Video
http://www.youtube.com/watch?v=0MMttNrig4I

World Healing ~ World Peace
Poetry 2014
www.worldhealingworldpeacepoetry.com

World Healing ~ World Peace Now

William S. Peters, Sr.

Inner Child Enterprises, ltd.
www.iaminnerchild.com

Table of Contents

Poetry

Table of Contents . . . *continued*

Table of Contents . . . *continued*

Epilogue   113

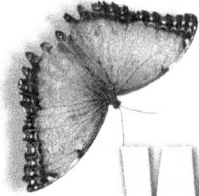

World Healing
World Peace

www.worldhealingworldpeacepoetry.com

World Healing World Peace Poetry

2014

Volume II

inner child press, ltd.

One word at a time, we as writers, deciphered our affect towards change for the basic principles of humanity. Through this collaborative effort, the initiative moves into the hands of our leaders, the diplomats of our freedoms, well-being, and peace. Whether they choose to page beyond the cover, and appreciate a literate world for change is now up to them.

Diane Sismour

Aquarius Khan

My name is Aquarius Khan (nee James Whaley). I grew up in New York City. Attended Hillcrest High School in Jamaica, Queens. As far as my formal education, it ended with receiving my G.E.D.

I was raised Christian- my father- Catholic, my mother- Baptist. She passed away when I was 15, he, when I was 18. The next 24 years was a combination of light and darkness. I adhere to the Book of Proverbs insistence on pursuing knowledge and wisdom- studied Western and Eastern theologies, immersed myself in hundreds of very well-researched books attended countless lectures and seminars but still couldn't escape the realities of my environment. I became addicted to drugs (now have 8 months clean time)- the years 2000-2010 held 3 prison sentences for me (all drug-related)- and finally this year completed my first poetry manuscript (as yet unpublished)- this piece I submit is entitled DISCIPLE- it is an expression not only of spirituality, but of culture as well.

https://www.facebook.com/aquarius.khan.37

1

DISCIPLE

Must we build a new school and temple?
Must we break the ground and the walls?
Who let demons inside the gates?
People, answer me when I call
Quiet my mind for meditation-
Beyond a storm of multiple disasters
If there be gods among you-
Have you seen the libraries of your masters?
It's been said that knowledge is power
Around what does the world of men turn?
What speaks in the movement of the stars?
Let me share with you what I've learned
Some mystery your teachers left hidden-
Having to do with Lucifer's ghost
Do preachers speak of a secret forbidden?
A masquerade with an invisible host
Let them wonder what force created us
There are ashes beneath the snow
For us to unite our divided tribes-
Let us meet in the valley below
Yes- I am the darker brother
Do you already prepare my grave?
But I shall not be moved
Must I quest within for a savior?
Can't kill that which cannot die
Place your crown of thorns on my head
For God my Father and Goddess my Mother-
Can faith now raise the dead?
Now what shall become of our children?
When I cry- I cry for the youth
Perhaps all the gods require blood-
I pray for an alternate truth
If I was fire- I'd be the Sun
If I was light- I'd come from the East
And in the end- when all is said and done-
They'll know that I worked for peace
If I was a flower- I'd be a rose
If I was a bird- I'd be a dove
And in the end- when all is said and done-
They'll know that I worked for love

2

Denise Lyles – Cook

DENISE L. COOK, THE ORACLE ~ A prolific writer who brings the written word to life. She has recently won her second Spoken Word Billboard Award and is now considered the #1 Spoken Word/Poet Artist of the Year, 2013. Denise L. Cook, The ORACLE, has a Word for You: "all-ways remember to love yourself"

theoracle.cook@gmailcom

www.ReverbNation.com/TheOracle

A Man Of Peace And Commitment ~ Of Firm And Pure Belief

A man of Peace and commitment
Of pure and firm belief
Troubled by the ills of his country
And taking action
Concerned for the loss of faith
Suffered by so many
Yet undoubting in his trust in the power
Of a true relationship with God
Enveloped by the protection
Of the strength of his belief in God
Revered and honored with an insatiable search
For justice, fairness, and embodying what it is to be like Christ
Forever a child of God
A man of peace and commitment
Of firm and pure belief
A master of the dialogue of life and
The spirit of the human condition
A champion for those who would not fight
For those who could not fight
By example and pure boldness he stands for God
By word he speaks to the consciousness of God
By deed he challenges others to step up to the calling of God
By love he shows the world how to give and receive the love of God
By choice he is a man of God
Cardinal Christian Wiyghan Tumi
Archbishop of Douala, Cameroon is
A man of peace and commitment
Of firm and pure belief

Ron Konstantin

Ron Konstantin aka "Mithrilweaver," Is an activist, singer, songwriter, poet, spoken word performance artist, and voice actor. He is 41 years old, and lives in Abilene, Texas.

ron1kon@hotmail.com
https://www.reverbnation.com/konstantinmithrilweaver

The Massacre

"Fade In"

Forever shall I recall the day

The day my spirit within my soul fell

My heart skipped a beat when I heard tell.

I heard of the elementary school massacre...

Of the killing field

Brought upon messenger

Driven by a black wind

Of deeds that should never have been.

Now, some expressed confusion,

But I knew exactly what to do.

Some said that things should be canceled

and silence is the best response.

but, BUT...

These are the times ...

The times in the course

Of the lives of men and women alike.

Where we show our mettle.

The value of the simple state of being

A human being

This is a time when those voices now silenced

cry for a voice among those who remain.

This is the very time

When a voice of reason is needed the most.

A sickness has covered this land,

this country, this world we all have to share..

It has become stained

Stained with blood of the innocent

What causes someone to kill

Women children complete strangers

That have done them no wrong?

What is the source of the obscenity

The madness that brings the sadness?

Where does it start? where does it begin?

It starts with you and me, my friend.

It is time we become our brother's keeper

And once again bring about awareness.

So write, speak, and pass on the words

That will champion this truest of causes.

We are the bards,

We are the voices

We are the poets,

The word smiths...

and the world needs us.

They await ...

YOU!

"Fade Out"

Jen Walls

Jen Walls is a celebrated and popular international global poetess that speaks directly inside a universal language of love. She believes life's sacred ceremony is capable of making a preserving peace through love. Jen is a writer, nature lover, ceremonial vocalist, and lives with family in Saint Paul, Minnesota.

Contact Jen at: writegift@msn.com and www.facebook.com/jen.walls.7

LOVE'S PEACE

Our soul will forever dance,
where time does only break.
Setting free inside adventuring,
we'll bend, burst and twist.

We'll splash to swim in ocean's tides,
to fall as waves, gently dropping away.
Going deeper within heart's joys,
we'll find our soul's surrendering.

On beatitudes of a lonesome galaxy,
go each celestial breath we'll make.
Birthing in stars that shine twinkling's,
we'll live in light's unending flame.

To forever lift up all hope to keep,
as love surely will find its way to stay.
Expanding the lover's light, we will continue.
We'll be the peace that has come to remain!

Christena AV Williams

Christena AV Williams is a young Jamaican poet and Author of newly published collection of poetry, "Pearls among Stones." This book can be found via the online bookstore blurb http://www.blurb.com/b/4148458- pearls-among-stones.

She is a radical thinker and writer and is not afraid to speak her mind and this poet is featured in international anthologies, Magazines online, Anthologies for charities, blogs, blog talk radios, literary sites and the local newspaper Gleaner.

She can be contacted via email : williams.christena@yahoo.com

Truth is Peace

The truth about peace is not to be delusional internalized
As world-peace means perfection
I wish for some peace, has I know the hearts of man
Do not get me wrong
I would dream of world peace but I am not a fool
Nor am I naïve to reality
So to make it clear and be fair
I want peace to reign at the maximum degree
In every corner of earth
I wish to walk in places with a peace of mind without fear
With love and protruding care
Speak the truth
Live truth
Be truth.
As it will resonate as an emblem of love and peace
Whatever a man thinketh so is he
For one to be healed one must revolutionize a man's thought
Remove the graffiti and zinc fences
Remove the mask of disguises
Teach love
Teach peace
Live it
So everyone may know of it.
The passion of your heart should propel it
Your art should showcase
Write and paste
Become the gallery of it
The truth about peace is not to be delusional internalized.

Mutha Wit Wisdom

Eye Am Mutha Wit Wisdom, a forty eight year old grandmother an Ordained Minister with Universal Life Church Ministries; developing a non profit organization, designed to decrease human suffering, by addressing and resolving physical, emotional, mental, and spiritual challenges, using Universal Laws to heal from a mind, body, soul, and spiritual foundation.

https://www.facebook.com/muthawit.wisdom

http://www.universalwomb.com/

The Miracle

One day, eye went looking for Peace in the world
what eye found were fragmented pieces of my soul
barren wastelands that were once rainforest
desserts that were were once oasis of Savannah's
the dry bones of souls that no longer walked the Earth
that's when eye began to weep for what once was
then a still quiet voice, whispered in the deepest part of me
why do you weep over what you had lost, and now have found
now that you are aware of your connection to the outside World
you can gather the unconditional energy of love, from the fragments
awaken each cell in your conscious being, enough to generate Self Love
with the advent of Self Love, everything changes
a chaotic world... becomes... a World of Peace

How does this miracle happen... eye asked in awe of what was said
Self Love has the ability to see, know, and believe its Cosmic Connection
it empowers the self, to know that it is made from the same natural energies
that formulate the stars, the milky way, the galaxy, the sands, the rainforest
the dessert, the plants, the animals, the birds, the fish, the seen and the unseen
when there is noticeable imbalance, it is because of a lack of Self Love
that lack is called fear...the frequency of fear...shatters World Peace into pieces
only Self Love, which is the original frequency, can give Birth to the hope of Peace
We are all a necessary component of that frequency
cultivate and achieve Self Love, and you will cultivate and achieve World Peace

Namaste

Sujan Bhattacharyya

Literary Activity, Poetry, Short Story, Essay basically in Bengali language and also in English.

Published Books

NISHKRANTO OKSHAR (Emerged Letters) - a book of poetry in Bengali

SHOBDER VALOBASA (Love of words) - same

14

Destiny Peace

Bugles have so far echoed in the sky,

Walls have fetched solitary reaping

Winnowing oneness from the being.

An ancient mariner traverses the path

Down the pages as history covers -

From the battlefield of Troy

To the bombardments coming.

None knows, whose blood is he shedding,

None knows, where the victorious crown

get its final nest.

Still the war is waged.

Let's move to war

A bitter, but a transient one;

Let us strike the marching drum

To warn the enemy in the front.

Let us all rise our hands

Let us all open our lips

Let us all wage the war

Leaving the bugle, to search for the flute.

Teresa E. Gallion

Teresa E. Gallion has published in numerous journals and anthologies. She has a chapbook, Walking Sacred Ground, a CD, On the Wings of the Wind and two books, Contemplation in the High Desert and Chasing Light.

You may preview her work at the websites noted below

http://bit.ly/1aIVPNq and http://bit.ly/13IMLGh

Pondering Peace

It is easy to fight and kill
and reuse all the old paradigms,
but takes courage to meet and greet in brotherhood.
We cannot conquer with flesh and metal.
That simply feeds the recycle bin of destruction
and never ending violent storms.
Arrogance makes every group believe
they will rise above annihilation.
The same radiation that kills your brother
will eventually consume you.
Negative affiliations must be removed.
You cannot reach your lake of serenity
paddling in greed, hate and anger.
Surrendering these deadly weapons gives
inner tranquility a chance. It is only then
you may spread harmony beyond your heart.
Every person has the potential to pursue nonviolence,
but many lack endurance to walk the peace road.
Are you willing to change the menu?
Taste the flavor of nonviolent fruit,
eat the salad of forgiveness, savor the dessert of love
and digest humanity healing in a pool of unity.

Simone Weber

My name is Simone Weber. I'm married and have two kids. I'm a writer and live in Germany.

Pain

You've been lucky, when you've been a child?
Or more like inside quiet outside wild?
Down-hearted and lucky at same time,
Your formerly happy eyes lost their shine.
You're screaming for help deep inside,
The wish to escape you have to hide.
Your true feelings – you're the only one who know,
Not allowed to tell anyone, not allowed to show.
Feeling alone, although your friends surrounding you,
You're needing a break, but you can't do.
You have to be always on the run,
For peoples entertainment, for peoples fun.
Your heart is so sad, although your face smiles,
Your body is tired, although you have to walk a million miles.
What you're thinking, but never said loud,
Is driving me crazy and makes me wanna shout!
My ability to help is restricted, even though I'd love to change,
Maybe I can lend an ear, even if we're strange.
Ever since I've known you I supported in every way,
I never thought of the price you had to pay.
I don't come along with all of your pain,
It seems to explode right into my brain.
If you ever want to open your soul – thoughts to share,
Please let me know – I ever will be there.
What it comes down to is, I don't have the words to explain,
How painful for me it is to see your pain.
My whole consideration I give to you,
It's not just a saying, I do mean it true!
Links contact and website: Simone-Weber-Buecher.de

Tiffany D. Glover

Tiffany D. Glover, a.k.a. "Jayne Phlow," is a 40 year-old single mother of a 14 year-old son, T'Zhean. She's been writing poetry for 25 years and performing for roughly 11 years. Her first book of poetry, "Get a Grip: Spilled Ink from my Soul," is due out March 2014.

THE REASON FOR EVERY SEASON

So the Christmas decorations are coming down,
And the New Year is close at hand,
And once again you've done your duty
By showing love to your fellow man.
You fed the homeless, you waved and smiled,
And showed tons of tender-loving care,
And while all that's great in representing the season,
Will it stick for the rest of the year?
You see, it's so much easier to feel all warm and fuzzy
With all the bright, shiny lights in your face
But as the seasons change, so do most attitudes
As everyone retreats back to their own space.
Gone are all of the "glad tidings of great joy,"
Gone are all the conversations started out of the blue,
And like our most comfy underwear, we easily put back on the mentality
Of "I'll do me…..so you do you."
How are we supposed to be a blessing like that?
How do we expect to be blessed like that?
How do we expect to really see God's goodness
If we remain secluded in our shells like that?
You never know who's meant to cross your path
Needing their soul to be touched.
Sometimes the simplest words or even a hug
Have the power to do so much.
So as you once again write out your New Year's Resolutions,
Start with one that may not be quite as hard.
Before you can try to affect change in other parts of our world,
First start in your own backyard.

Bob Strum

Dr. John R. Strum aka Bob is a retired Forensic Psychiatrist, avid writer and Published Author. He resides in Coffs Harbour, New South Wales. You may find his books at the links below

http://www.innerchildpress.com/dr-john-r-strum.php

STEAM OVER HOT SPRINGS

Nothing has changed
Since I went to sleep.
The author of my dreams
Has changed the script.
The demons and phantoms
Have stayed at home,
Letting me
Sleep in peace.
The Sun is slow in rising.
Like a rabbit going down a hole.
But soon he will arise
In triumph.
Another day will begin.
I have awoken
In quiet optimism.
I feel love rising
Like a steam
Over hot springs.
No only
The hot springs inside me
But those existing
All over the world.
It could be
I delude myself.
I feel a surge of hope.
The rampant Darwinian Demon
May yet be conquered.
And peace may spring forth
Like Flowers in spring.

Stuart Marshall

stuartirvingmarshall is a lifelong lover of poetry and has been writing it for the past sixteen years. His latest work, Youth, Struggle, Wisdom: The Journey to Epsilon, will be available in January 2014.

The Sweetest Taste

There are battles fought every day
unseen unheard with no smoke no fires
no broken bodies or rubble to stumble through
no blood but the lifeblood of the soul
that which struggles to live on
find a purpose in the life given
find that peace that peace that passeth all understanding
the healing beyond bandages
beyond the salve of a smile
a quiet moment when
no bombs fall
when men women and children
cease their painful cries
where the hand reaching out
the hands reaching out
are both yours and mine
a mutually synchronized healing
feeling of warmth and joy
beyond space heaters and bars of chocolate
we starve not for sweets
but the sweet taste of peace
and the moment when
the joy begins and the healing
shows its mark of love
through love that's all about love
and nothing else
the beginning of peace and healing
for nothing else matters or will ever matter
as much.

Su(e) Diyg

Su(e) Nia Diyg is primarily a visual artist, but began writing poetry briefly in college, and then more seriously from 1998-2006. In 2013, she began a friendship with poet stuartirvingmarshall, leading to their collaborative work in poetry.

C'monPeople Now

Spendin'DaSummer of my 11thYear singin'

C'monPeople, now playin' on the radio, with my family

drivin' through Slashed&Burned downtown DC.

Bringin' Betty Back2HerFuture in Georgetown...

tryin'a MakeSense of NotThatRay's bloody Memphis deed.

WatchedInShock as Sirhan'sShot

heard RoundDaWorld made Bobby bleed.

SundayFunnies asked the OnlyQuestion

i would EverNeed...

AnswerMe: Seriously, why be jealous of the NaturalTan...

Is melanin the MarkOfHam's sin?!

NO!!! Li'lAbner knew...& even then,

EvenThen i did, too...ain't he JustAMan??

C'monPeople, now...Smile on YourBrothers,

GetReady! Teach YourSister well

(y)our Mother'sHell. i was OldOfSoul though

YoungOfBlood: been helpin' out since 8YearsOld.

At 14, moved to Memphis where da ManOfBlack was seen

as BogieMan of children's NightmareScream.

Would the hatred EverEnd? Would we live Dr. King's GreatDream?

It would take More'n40Years to see the fruit of his DCMarch of '63

and in Less'nHalf a decade, his MartyrDom in Memphis, Tennessee

and in Less'nHalf another, i FoundMySelf confusedly

tryin'a MakeSense of why the RacistIdeology

made ItSelfFelt in school, in church, in EveryPlace a sin

to hang with people with a DifferentColor skin.

This day, the 12:05 of the Year13,

plus 2KYears after ChristOnEarth had been…

a Souldier left us. What a WonderfulWorld he'd seen

rise from the ashes of Botha's apartheid hell…

With white DeKlerk, Mandela taught SouthAfrica's children well:

Imprisoned 2ScoreYears&7, a LuckyNumber when

the Millennium'sTurn was due, minus 10—within 4Years,

he was ElectedPresident. In 5 years, what'd he do?

Forgave those WhoseBiggestSin was hatin' him

for the RichEarth's dark brown color of his skin.

Headed a Government of NationalUnity—all 3

PoliticalParties worked together on policy: rich still so,

but Poor&Colored now were free to see:

in the MindOfGod, no ColorLine parts you & me.

C'monPeople now, smile on YourBrother

everybody GetTogether, try & LoveOneAnother

right now…right now…RightNow.

Satwik Mishra

Satwik is an Engineer by education, an entrepreneur by profession and an author by passion. He was born on 5th July,1991 in Purnea, Bihar (India) and at present is in his final year of B.tech degree course at VIT University, Vellore (Tamilnadu).With creative vein inside, Satwik always tries to run his blood actively for doing something unique and innovative.

Religion

Looking at world's endless rage,

Not just today, but from ancient days.

Finally I talked to God,

Over my unbounded frustration.

Charging him up for being culprit,

Behind this intense destruction.

I was not ready at all,

To fell down with any renounce.

Even God dint show unexpectedly,

Any argument in his response.

Innocently he laughed and answered-

" It's not me,

But you people on the earth.

Who named a single entity,

With different names.

Who framed various religions,

Just to play all dirty games.

Who keep on fighting unreasonably,

Having God to throw all blames.

Think and realise all these facts,

You will to find a reason to shame."

Leaving me speechless behind.

Renee Yvonne Burgess

Who am I? I am a remix of myself, with original vocals and sampled background beats.

My inspiration has been provided by the circumstances and stimuli that compose my surroundings I'm a montage collage.

WE WERE CARVED FROM THE SAME TREE

Purification
Provides our soul's antidote
To this world's toxins!
Our backs are outstretched to support family equilibrium
Bracing ourselves for the challenges of struggles to come
Our stance is immovable, as we are intertwined by destiny
To ensure group survival
Holding hands in a circle, our rainbow hearts pound in unison
To ancestral rhythms and eternal vibrations
Co-dependently pumping the life blood of the past, present and future
With each beat, we inherit the intergenerational legacy of wisdom
Preservation of culture guarantees the kaleidoscope reincarnation of hope
As we leap over life's obstacles, we travel in a herd
Collectively catching those who stumble over hurdles
And fighting daily battles to rescue our precious young
By fending off predators who prey on their innocence
And devour concentrated blossoming ambition
We clung desperately to the same roots
Were nourished by the same ravenous love
Breathed the same labored breath
Cried the same salty bitter tears
And chased the same passionately proud peacock dreams
Banishing the grey negative energy that destructively swallows whole tender souls
For we were carved from the same tree!
Peace brands open hearts
I'm world peace and world healing

LOVE TRANSCENDS HATRED!

Oswald Okaitei

Oswald Okaitei is a native of Osu Kinkawe, a town in Accra- the capital of Ghana. He is a graduate of University of Cape Coast. He had his Senior and Junior High education at Presbyterian Boys' SHS and Seven Great Princes Academy respectively. As a child, he showed great interest in the theatre arts and his exceptional talent saw him featured in a lot of stage and screen plays.

His literary works include 'Nkrumah Might Be Right!', 'Who Stole The Casket?', The X'mas Gift. (Plays). ' A Wreath To Awoonor!', 'Songs Of Condolence To Tacloban' and 'ON 24TH JULY' (In memory of Prof Atta Mills) (Poetry). With the exception of 'A Wreath To Awoonor!', the rest are soon to be launched.

AN EPISTLE TO SOUTH SUDAN

Souls
Are gripped by the claws of fear
And tears!...
They flood cheeks amidst screams and weary...

O thou youngest
Of Africa
And
Surely, the seemingly last of mother earth

Why art thou
Sought
The
Path towards the inner core of hell?
Why scar
Thy
Shore of wealth
With the bloods of thy innocent souls?

Did
You Fall apart
From the feed of your mother's breast
To fall apart?

Awake
From the slumber of shame
And
Seek the path to exalt thy name in glory!

Where art thou
Reached?
Why
Do you surge, in your adolescence, unto the shores of the follies?

Have you not fed
The nuts
Of your tympanic and the retina of your eyes
With
The evolutionary traits of the guns' topple?

If thou
Art slept thy eyes to the woes of war
Awake them...
Hence, you set a blaze to suffer the pains of hell
Before cometh, hell!

Why slay
The sweetness of dialogue
To log
In into the roaring dehumanizing war's arms?

Awake!
Awake your sleeping conscience
Lest you join the follies
And remark,...'Art thy known!'

Dr. Nachiketa Bandyopadhyay

Dr. Nachiketa Bandyopadhyay(1960) is a Zoologist, currently serving as a Registrar at Sidho Kanho Birsha University, Purulia, India. His research area are History of Arts, Science, Woman Studies, Cultural Studies and Environnment.

OM Shanti! Om Shanti!

In quest of comfort
How much, How much depletion
Earth is made up of Plastic
Oh Carbon Civilization!
Who made me Greedy?
Who made me Failed?
But man and matter non-dual
We the Custodian of our life

Truth is the Non-Violence
Ahimsa brings freedom
From hate, fear, Jealousy and the narrowness
Look the Earth, Everything enough for need
Look the earth, Everything little for Greed

Both the seeds from the same tree
Peace and Violence
Which you will sow and nurture
To cultivate inner peace
Your role model is Tree
Who is Tolerant with the intolerant
And mild among the Violent

Tony Roberts

I am a 53 year old veteran, left leg amputation. I have had 54 surgeries, and many months of hospital stays. I have had much pain and heartache, and needed an escape. I started writing a lot of poetry, and this allowed me to show my heart to others.

Peace

Peace leads the way.
As we're hand in hand.
The love that is with us,
Could cover this land.

Peace flows through the mountains,
And then becomes streams.
It helps flowers grow,
In all of our dreams.

Peace passes through forests,
Just like a wild deer.
Although he is eating,
He knows when you're near.

Peace can stay with us,
And rise up above.
But it must have food,
It lives off of love.

Peace is what helps us,
To get through the day.
Just always remember;
There's no other way.

Mark Avery

I go by Mark Avery. My full name is Mark A Bester. Born and raised on Chicago's south side. I can be reached at bester1969@gmail.com.

I have been Writing on and off since the age of nineteen, but took a true interest when I tried my hand at the music industry in the late 80's early 90's. I have some formal education in literature and creative writing due to my education at Harold Washington College located in downtown Chicago. I didn't complete my education in writing, but continued my education in the technical field graduating with a degree in electronics. I took a hiatus from writing when I got married. It's been fourteen years since I've written anything, but if felt so good placing those words on paper. It's been a year since my divorce and I find writing is a release for me and helps me focus on life again. I plan to continue on this journey in hopes of writing a fictional novel. During that time I plan on continuing scripting poetry on any and all subjects that cross my mind.

Disease called Hate

Thinking about how deadly the disease hate is. Hate has claimed more lives than all viruses combined. Just look throughout the history of the world and see how many lives have been taken due to direct and indirect contact with this disease called hate. Religion is suppose to be about love, but as you look through the pages of holy doctrines you read about wars, murders, senseless brutality and death due to this disease called hate.

Our lord and savior was a victim, casualty of this disease called hate. It's often said that the heart is conditioned and was made to radiate love, but when it's poisoned by this disease called hate, it turns black and cold. I truly believe that love can conquer all, but the when hand of violence rears its ugly head and you have a choice to make. You either try to let loves light shine through, or take up arms and defend yourself.

Nowadays we fight hatred with more hatred which only leads to death and destruction. I know it's a dream, but I pray for the day we can all live in harmony with one another but before that day comes I truly think that this disease called hate will destroy us all.... Sorry, not too much of a positive message but just how I'm feeling about this disease called hate.

Sylvia Ramos Cruz

Sylvia Ramos Cruz loves words for their sounds and their ability to distill a personal experience into a shared humanity. She believes poetry can not only inspire spiritual ruminations but also move us to action on behalf of the Universe. She lives amidst the beauty of the American Southwest.

Countdown at Fukushima Daiichi

Never doubt that a small group of thoughtful, committed people can change the world.
Margaret Mead 1901-1978.

Fifty years ago a shy marine biologist

saw the dangers DDT and other chemicals

concocted to help humans live better lives

presented to all life. Her 1962 Silent Spring

spoke so loudly even President JFK listened.

While she quietly underwent radiation to control

metastatic breast cancer, Rachel Carson heard

the silence of birds and inspired a movement

that birthed the Environmental Protection Agency.

Thirty-five years ago Lois Gibbs, a 27-year-old

housewife, mobilized a choir of voices demanding

change. They took hostages until government

officials including President Carter took action.

the people of Love Canal were moved away from

the toxic landfill on which their children's school

sat and which had already damaged the chromosomes

of thirty percent of the town. The Superfund to clean

hazardous waste sites was born on that site.

Two-and-a-half years into the disaster
men and machines rake the soil, pull the weeds
disgorge them into row after row of black bags
that are left to sit plump and radiant in the sun
waiting for purification.

Two-and-a-half years into the disaster
white-coveralled men in orange helmets,
plastic gloves, booties and respirator masks
file in and out of melted nuclear reactors like mutant
necrophory ants removing the dead from their nests.

Two-and-a-half years into the disaster
groundwater gurgles its way into contaminated
pools where spent fuel rods lie like sleeping giants
ready to wake and pounce if not kept cool enough;
quarantined water seeps silently out of steel tanks
bypassing concrete barricades to flow into the Pacific—
a current catastrophe spreading world-wide
in seawater, rain, fish and birds.

Two-and-a-half years into the disaster
there is silence in Futaba, Fukushima, Japan.

Gabrielle Streck is a poet and writer.

For my " Angel ", Marion
Tribute to a dear friend and poet

You came to me one autumn day

a random meeting I would say

There was no business for us to do,

but our spirits connected like glue

For years now we've only "talked" online you know,

because you lived near the beach

and I, near the snow.

And we did not always see eye to eye

but when you had troubles, I too, would cry.

You, the one who would never judge

and I'm sure you've never held a grudge.

But my opinions you could not always sway

Many times, for me, to God, you would pray.

But when I hurt, I knew you were at my side

And for my losses I knew you cried.

Each other's joys together we shared

For one another we always cared.

And if one day we could not meet online

I knew you were hoping for my day to be fine.

That August morn', her waves came your way

I prayed that you had not chosen to stay

I prayed to God that you were "safe 'n' sound"

Sadly, my prayers were not answered, I found.

The ocean that you lived so near

Had taken the life of my friend so dear.

So often, still, for you, I will cry

But go on each day, for you, I must try.

Just weeks ago, I teased you,

when it was your time you'd fight

neither of us knowing that so soon

the angels would take you in flight.

I was not ready to lose the Marion I adore

But I know, God must have needed you more.

This poem is for my dear friend Marion, who lost her life

to Katrina's wrath on August 29th.

For Marion Beckendorf Stearns (June,'49-Aug '05)

Raja Williams

I am Raja, a free spirited American woman with a name from India that means king. My name has helped shape me into my own unique being through this life's journey. I walk the path of spirituality connecting with people, animals and nature. My insights are shared through my poetry and thoughts.

www.Rajasinsight.com

Mother Earths Echo

Can you hear me . . .
Can you hear the whisper of a gentle breeze
The roar of the winds
The crashing of the surf onto the beach
The arrival of seawater upon your feet
The gurgle of the rivers water tumbling over rocks
The pitter-patter of rain dropping from the sky
Thunder crashing, animal calls . . .
Can you hear at all?
Our land is screaming out to us
But we are not listening
We are ignoring the cries of our suffering planet
Losing connection to Mother Nature
Brought on by Urban Sprawl
We have lost the purity of the air we breathe!
We have lost the purity of the water we need to drink!
We endanger ourselves through the food we eat!
Don't you think it's time to get in sync?
What would Mother Earth say if she could talk to me?
She would tell us . . .
Learn to listen inwardly . . .
Hear the sounds of the earth
In your very own heart beat
Take time to expand and learn
Connect Spiritually with our land
Reach out a helping hand to those in need
Be in sync with the world
Because the world outside of you
Slowly transforms . . .
And becomes the world inside of you.
We are one, we are the world.

Kay Salady

Kay Salady is a poet residing in Arizona, USA. Kay is read internationally, having published works in America as well as India. She has been a featured author for Global Light Minds Magazine, The Arachneed, as well as the Global Peace Journal. Her passion is freedom of expression and unity.

I'd Paint Peace

If I could paint a masterpiece
I'd paint a world that echoed peace
Upon the wind and across the land
Inside the heart of every man

I'd paint a sky of clearest blue
Where rainbow wishes all came true
With fluffy clouds that gathered dreams
Within their silver-crested seams

I'd dip my brush in paint so pure
To paint a land that felt secure
Where children in her bosom lay
In fields of green to gently play

There would be golden daffodils
Atop the rolling amber hills
Where shadows of their unity
Could somehow set the captive free

A splash of paint upon the page
Had run the river toward the sage
Who dared to give the world release
By painting words that offered peace

Lindsey Rhodes

Lindsey Rhodes is an inspiring poet who is currently an administrator of The Writers' Connection group. As a former military veteran; he sought to writing as an outlet to deal with the rigmarole. He is also a part of many writing groups on various social media outlets. He is originally from New Orleans but now resides in Ohio with his girlfriend and his two children.

Life Support

Unwarranted damage bruising her soul

Years of abuse is taking its toll

Lost is the connection to it all

While the masses await for the final downfall

Of a matriarch who has done no harm

Mortally wounded by the blasts; ring the alarm

Transformed into a shell of herself

Stripped, poked, drilled, and prodded of her wealth

Clinging on by a thread; while being confined to life support

Dreams of a harmonious ending; but the vision is too cloudy to distort

Loretta Hardrick

Loretta L. Hardrick is the fourth born to Jammie L. Black Sr. and Vermelia M. Black, born in Oklahoma raised in church, began writing poetry at nine and singing publically at eleven. She is a singer/songwriter; author, writer and poet, by nature; a mother and wife by choice, Nanna to eight grandchildren; passionately.

For a complete bio visit her website: http://www.apoetsmusic.com/.

Closed Eyelids Equal Darkness

I might as well be dead and in my grave or laying in a casket or become enslaved because I am trying to express to you a serious injustice to the entire world of leaders to whom we have entrusted. Entrusted our lives, our dreams and our souls; signed away our rights to equality at the voting polls. Ears are full of wax because they choose and refuse to listen, listen to the cries from the blood stained streets that tell of the human death toll by the loved ones; gone missing.

Look to the north, the south, the east and the west; can you not see the trials of our nations that have left the countries in distress. Misfortune and mishaps are occurring each and every day but you continue to strut boldly to avoid hearing what we, "the people," have to say. With your eyelids closed you can't see anything but darkness accompanied with the shallowness that darkness brings.

Closed Eyelids Equal Darkness, as dark as the midnight sky. Closed eyelids equal tear drops that fall to the pages of a dreadful lullaby. The pages are missing, what's on this earth that really matters. Stop all the violence in our streets; stop all the families that are being shattered. You've taken prayer out of the schools, abolished the golden rule, disrespected the law and want to blame us; oh naw.

You cannot see with your eyelids closed, you were made to breathe through the nostrils of your nose. Some things come naturally, to some but not to all, most of us have sense enough to get back up when we stumble or fall. Open your eyes and see what is taking place, from God's perspective it's a sinful disgrace.

Closed eyelids equal darkness not light and just because you keep your eyes closed doesn't mean you're doing what is right. We must be held accountable for our actions every day. We need to be responsible for the wrongs we have done and not try and run the other way.

Some nights, I lie in my bed and just cry because of the numerous injustices that get approved which cause another human being to die. When you exist in the darkness, you can't see where you're going; you're tripping over wounded bodies, all bloodied without even knowing. Where will it stop, where do we draw the line? Procrastinations equal; "not even trying!"

Closed eyelids equal darkness which means you are blind and if you practice it long enough, it becomes a habit which equals denying. See with your eyes and not with your tongue, wisdom becomes knowledge if you know the words to the song. Sing of a time when we have peace to receive, sing of a time when we once again can believe. Believe in the laws of the land that are governed by a few, just because you delegate doesn't mean you don't have to abide by them too.

Closed eyelids equal darkness and darkness leads to despair; despair leads to restless desperation which equals the electric chair. Wake up from your sleeping there is work to be done; we will never win the battle if you don't recognize that there is one to be won. Motion upward with your eyeballs and your eyelids will open wide. Keep looking up because in Christ, is where our strength lies. Look to the hills from whence comes our help if we lean on, the Father and put him first then and only then can we take a backseat to self; "self," keeps us bogged down and it keeps, getting in the way. Get behind yourself, come let us pray, now is the right time for closed eyelids as now they can see; "The light!"

Lady Silk

Lady Silk was featured on several blogtalkradio shows and has performed exclusively at the Inspired Word. Author of Silk Elements "A Poets Origin". She will be releasing her next two books, Breaking Boundaries "Confessions of a Mad Poet and 3 Generations Thralldom a Novella on Slavery early 2014.

Omnipotent

In the name of love

I swarmed through oceans of mysteries and drank fire and brimstones

While dancing upon Mount Everest

I found the magic in the reasons

That took us outside the realm of impossibilities

Where many failed to succeed

I spent hours rediscovering and protecting myself

Afraid of indecisive thoughts

All the while searching for definitive answers

I was lodged in a place that sheltered me

Magnificently hidden, I shined

While other stars burned out

I transported thousands of electrical currents spontaneously

That multiplied ignition

While your reverence surround me

I stood atop the sun and slowly drifted amidst the storm

Casting enlightenment

While humility radiated from core

I crossed a spiritual bridge and made love

In the sanctuary of endless visions

While birthing bright stars continuously

I searched for boundaries

Where, knowledge was supposed to be applied and

Where life had no limits

I watched people searching the world

Wandering blindly through darkened streets

While cities cried out in vain

I crossed a river and its waters contained

The bitterness of stolen memories

While the waves sang shamelessly

I cast out their dreams containing the demons

That disbursed lies' like dragonflies

While bitter hearts bled truth

We as people, assume World Power as the ultimate power

Where we endlessly undervalue its reverence and political standings

Mankind continues to remain unyielding and unaffected

Whereas I swarmed through oceans of mysteries

While drinking fire and brimstones,

I wondered, In the name of love

Are we not our brothers' keepers?

Shihi Venus

Greetings, I am Shihi Venus, a passionate shy, an eccentrically poetic writer. I am a guiding light for humanity of peaceful plans and solutions, to be executed for the world to heal and live in peace.

Poetry to me, is my life expressed from the inside and out my life thoughts, experiences and future journey in this world today.

https://www.facebook.com/suynshyn

Give Peace A Chance

There's danger of human and animal

Wild life becoming extinct

New world slavery and human Starvation and Trade

Leadership starts within ourselves

Time waits for no one

We must begin again ...no one person

Can judge another if that person

Isn't putting in time for humanity's

Change in our lifetime

Let's try Peace 4 once in this world

Although John Lennon wrote "Give

Peace a Chance for the calling of Global Peace into 1970's for the "Praising

American Anti Violence Pressure Group

I find thst this is still a war of all wars

Stronger hungering for World Healing

And World Peace Movement

And these years are years we're living

Dangerously...We need one another

All around the world I tire myself

Mentally and heartbreaks while I

Volunteer the neo-natal units of the

Childrens Hospital holding drug and

Abandoned babies whom doesn't know

What Love is...what do they know about

Peace...Love and Peace goes hand in hand and was formed from within us all

Of all the leaders and governmental authorities in control I would not believe

We live in times of "Blind Justice"

We can't stand by waiting for our

Brother and Sister to pull us through

This is all up to me and you

I can't just stand by and let this happen

I can't turn the other cheek on these evil

Killings, hunger, new world slave trades and starvation ...to disagree with what's

Going on in the streets ....actions of neglect, some from the government on

Specific issues choosing opinions agreed by our constitution who would

Carr about giving Peace A Chance,

Love A Chance, life A Chance and the

World A Chance...We Have To Heal

The World To Make It A Better Place ,

By Teaching, Loving , Giving, and

Starting it within...

Diamond Ryan

The Authorship Of My Pen

I started writing at a young age. It came to me as a gift at a point in life where I could actually remember being able to officially call it "writing". It all began in my junior high school years, while attending Walton Jr. High. There was a keen scholarly mistress at the school I attended, whose name escapes me just now, who would become the first to encourage me. It is to that teacher's humble and giving legacy that I lend my literary.

I don't define or confine myself to or by the 'road posts' strewn along the way in life... They are merely guides put in place and marked as help. A testament of others who have traveled that same path towards their own dreams. Who have courageously faced many diversities in pursuit of all the options this world holds. Leaving behind torn little pieces of fabric on a twig in this wooded forest called life. Knowledge. Wisdom. Lore.

http://www.amazon.com/DiamondRyan/e/B008MOOLQA/ref=ntt_athr_dp_pel_1

DEAD BY BLACK ASSASSINATION

Another Mommy, but no daddy,
Families lost in the system,
The system fails badly.
Welfare, ain't fair.
It was created to get you nowhere.
It won't help you stand
And, if you fall, it won't help you up.
So you rob, steal and deal,
Even give up a little butt.
Just to feed your family...
Just to make the cut.
Babies hatching babies
Their lives corrupt.
By political black sell outs.
Sold out.
Telling little white lies...
In black robes,
And uniforms
Supporting false alibis
"To Protect And Serve"
Yeah, "their" influential ties.
Lies, lies, lies...
I can't stand "n****s and flies...
Meanwhile tykes are tempted
Their lives preempted
They get no sympathy,
No apathy, no empathy...
They are enslaved in the slavery of never being free
Ready to die for some dignity,
Now....
"What was the question?
Oh!
To be or not to be
But at what cost to society?
How do we ever become free
When the false reality, is all we see?

It's all we see...
It's all we see.
Sinning and grinning
The whole world spinning
That's all the little babies see.
Metalflake red, pimped out 'Caddie',
With "dusters"...
And, BOOM, BOOM, BOOM!
For cool daddy.
Setting the example of our people, behaving badly.
With their spinning wheels,
And big money deals
And the drug dealers, dealing deals
All 'gold up' in their grill.
Pumping out mad rap from behind the wheel
Vibrating fenders...
Mind and nerve benders...
That's just 'cause the music's so loud!
Old 'Gs' never die.
They just keep counting Benjamins and selling lies,
About what aint right, and what ain't real...
Teaching our young brothers
How to case and steal...
Can you feel me?!!!
A drug sting, then a drug bust
Lucky one's walk away in cuffs
Shots were fired at a cop,
Then one by one, they each one dropped.
Gold trim caskets to pine box coffin...
Gotta stop coming to these funerals so often.
Well... ashes to ashes and dust to dust
What don't shine ...will turn to rust.
Had fifteen minutes of fame,
Was on top of his game...
Then, Momma's 18 year investment …
Down the drain.
Like you didn't know....
Ill gotten wealth

Equals jail time... or drug deaths.
Look around you homeboy...
Ain't many of your homies left.
Living in sin everywhere you've been.
Hatred, jealousy, turf envy...
Ducking drivebys... by wannabes!
Pop! Pop! Pop!... Pop! Pop!
Five rounds fired...
Then R.I.P.!
"See Ya later Pooky"
"This is the way we roll!"
"Southside!"
(Written in white on the back of some homie's car window)
Even before the ink dries...
Another one dies.
Then another...
And another...
And another one dies.
We all so tired ya'll...
Of this... fightless fight.
Still....
Ol' "Hitman" just wanna catch the n*****
In his sight.
Then it's pay back time...
'Cause the money wasn't right.
Just one less brother,
Come sunrise.
Here...
Here's two copper pennies for two still eyes...
'Cause see...
They don't quit, 'til they end the shit.
Black genocide...
Killing from the inside...
Penny rich and stupid wise....
Trigger pulled...
The bullet flies...
A young black boy...
Slumps to the side.

The phones rings...
A mother cries.
The sad empty reflection is in her eyes
As she weeps for this child
That shouldn't have died...
Because...
He was one of the innocent ones...
Standing on the byside.
But, these dumb asses... they don't quit.
At the enemy's grave site
They'll sit and sit,
Waiting and wanting,
Wishing and daring... 'somebody'
To come on with it.
'Because another mother******'s got to be wasted
Behind this shit!'
At after burial barbques,
Processed and SCurl fools
In Asian store bought jewels...
Are leading sermons 'bout...
'How one should live or die..'.
Standing around smokin'
Blunt rolled tokin'
Talking 'bout...
"Somebody's" dead body....
Is gonna pay some dues.
Paying dues...
Paying dues...
Paying dues...
Well, you ain't gonna here the KKK "Sing da blues..."
Because... just another black brother is dead ya'll...
By Black assassination.
Stop the violence. Choose or Lose LIFE.

Janet P. Caldwell

Janet P. Caldwell is currently the COO of Inner Child, ltd., Humanitarian, Reiki Master, Poet, Published Author, *5 degrees to separation, Passages* and *Dancing Toward the Light . . . The Journey Continues,* many anthologies, magazines and more. To read more of Janet's work please visit the links below.

http://www.janetcaldwell.com/
http://www.innerchildpress.com/janet-p-caldwell.php
https://www.facebook.com/JanetPCaldwell

Peace Talks

Lay down your weapons
put your hatred aside
and just for a moment
think for yourselves
not parroting . . .
what someone else has said.

It is only the unknown
that is so frightening
the shadows that scare.

This concept . . .fear
that has stricken the hearts of men
when conversations have never begun
or have been carelessly withdrawn
is ludicrously inept.

Sit with me, let us converse, you will see
that we all want the same things
at least similarly
for our precious families
throughout this vast humanity.

The imagination can be a cruel master
and emotions may be acted on
and do not reveal the truth
of what is happening
when no-one is talking
except the political
brain – washing, big guns.

Our children suffer the most
there are generations
who have never experienced peace
and this is a sad state of affairs.
Don't we care ?

Do we name ourselves as good examples ?
Tell me now, I do not understand.
With the current legacy we're leaving
how will history record us ?
Are we proud of ourselves ?

For my sake and for yours
the sake of the innocents
I am opening my hands
letting go of who's right or wrong.
Though culturally different
aren't we the same ?

Love will take us there
leading to the exchange of ideas
understanding ideals
watch the healing begin.
Together we'll sing songs
of reconciliation
hand in hand in hand.

I don't know about you
but I do know that it begins with me.
I have taught my children
to love the Global Family.
Won't you join us
and give it a try ?

Take my hand in peace.
For I too . . . am your family
and just for this moment
let us think for ourselves
not parroting . . .
what someone else has said.

There is no trust more sacred than the one the world holds with children. There is no duty more important than ensuring that their rights are respected, that their welfare is protected, that their lives are free from fear and want and that they grow up in peace.
Kofi Annan

70

N. Owen Holme

N. Owen Holme is an American military veteran with several fiction and non-fiction articles published which, surprisingly, earned enough to purchase an exercise machine. He resides in Dallas, TX with his spouse and cat. The exercise machine is gathering dust and the author thinks that he may have been involved in writing for his own ego gratification and not for the material gain but has yet to reach a conclusion on his motives at this time.

https://app.heliumnetwork.com/heliumnetwork/viewPublicUserBio.sc?userNumber=6510 23

The Problem with Peace

Peace, if it were a card in the standard poker deck
would always be a 3 because the deuces, at times,
are wild, but never the 3's. Even the 3 of rods
or swords, given the tarot origins, are weak,
and even more significantly, dull and ordinary.
In many ways they are only there to round out
the deck. In pinochle, the 3's are not even a footnote.

Like the 3's, in some games such as poker,
peace has a chance at winning when chained
to other cards, other 3's or a low straight,
but the experienced gambler never bets heavy
in this instance...it loses too often. In other words,
peace is easily trumped.

Much has been proposed, in political narrative
and the philosophical and the fantasies of most
literature about a world without violence, and in this,
peace is at war with itself because it enters this conflict,
not as alternative, but as an antagonist and this is where
the concept fails at every level except the sentimental
because it disguises itself as a value exclusive of the game,
yet overtly challenges the face cards that it cannot match
within the game where it knows itself to be weak. A four
and wild deuce beat a pair of 3's every time.

If peace has any chance, the game and the deck need revision,
otherwise, you're still betting against the house
with a losing strategy and no one, especially the house,
has much sympathy for your effort. And if you are enamored
of the idea of an enduring world that knows no conflict,
I apologize for pointing out that you are taking a sauna
over the cesspool...it may feel soothing but you won't get clean.

Rajenda k. padhi

Rajendra k. Padhi at present working as lecturer in the Department of English in Women's College, Bargarh, Odisha has already published four volumes of poetry- THE LIVING TOUCH, O EARTH! by Alpha publications, New Delhi, SONGS OF VOID and SUNYATARA PRIYATAMA in Odiya in bilingual edition. THE DARK HOURS is his first English novel. His articles on education and literature in English and Oriya have been widely appreciated. Articles like "Inquest of True Education", "Lyric poetry of western odisha" "Regional literature – an overview", "Going off the track", "Frankenstein Monster", "where are we?", "Women's Colleges – A New Thrush" and many more have received high acclamation. He was born at padampur in the district of Bargarh, Odisha in 1963.

ROSES BLOOM IN THORNY-STEM

The sun comes out of empty space
Dispels darkness in its blessed light,
Persistently works for us till the dusk
Parting it yields a treasure rare.

The stars in chorus sing of dreams
Waking we discover a sea of hope,
We twinkle till the dawn of our goals
We fitly pull our little life to shore,

Born from the dark the moon glitters
Lights each shadow in its sombre flight,
Creep into buds of lily in kindly love
It shines in the night in silvery frame.

The ruddy stream comes out of rocky hill
Downward it moves on perilous ways,
Sings so sweet in accents of love flows
Gently in loud hymns finds sunlit-shore.

Winter in sighs of sadness on snowy lips
Withers the grass from its green spirit,
Gathers spring in her womb as child
So elating for flowers swaying in wind.

My steps move in the orbit of Earth
Glancing each goal so distant, so far,
Unceasingly I pray as a child of clay
See the roses blooming in thorny stem.

hülya n. yilmaz

hülya n. yılmaz, a college professor, has authored Trance, a collection of English, German and Turkish poems (published by Inner Child Press, ltd). Pastiche, Twist of Fate and Inner Child Magazine are platforms where her poems appeared first. Presently, she teaches full-time and writes poetry and prose.

Contact Link: hulyayilmaz19@yahoo.com
Website: http://dolunaylaben.wordpress.com

even time and space united

twelfth century Central Anatolia – cradle of civilizations
birthed Rumi, a poet of spirituality
amid teeming wars over religion and arms
he pled all colors of skin, worshippers of any shape or belief
called upon unity on behalf of humanity
he was neither the first nor the last to implore
the seed of homosapiens is the same at its core
the twentyfirst century might – Mandela's South African light
caressed him – Tolstoy, Picasso not far behind
nineteenth century Persia
labored Baha'u'llah
to wed world religions
Siddhartha Gautama donned India
in sixth century before Christ
with values of peace
liberating his devotees
from earthly agonies
doves led King to a North American glide
that twentieth century's potent ripples still in tranquil ebb and tide
guarding the tortured, those imprisoned, lynched
nurturing them all, Socrates kept vigil – though in poison of hatred
before Christ through Confucius the Golden Rule revived
alas! an ancient old wisdom had survived:
"Men's natures are alike, it is their habits that carry them far apart."
habits to arm, to discriminate
to abolish love, to nourish only those who hate
fossilized as heirlooms, resisted each age, firm not to abate
yet
even time and space prevailed to unite
for they had love's healing command on their side
at warp speed, the peaceful have become and multiplied

Gandhi
Dalai Lama, the 14th
Gorbachev
Walesa
Suu Kyi
Williams
Corrigan
Laroupe
Ali
Malala
Hanh
Chinmoy
Vivekananda
Wilberforce
Tutu
Jefferson
Wilson
Annan
Carter
Mother Teresa
they
we
he
she
you
i...

Saleh Mazumder

Md. Saleh Mazumder: born in 1st September 1985, from Dhaka Bangladesh, graduated in Business Information Technology. He is a business professional, published author of poetry books and anthologies. He is the featured poet of World Poetry Canada and International. He thinks poetry is a perfect media in which to express unspoken words for bringing the world together as one voice. And working together for a more peaceful and beautiful world that is ever becoming a better place to live!

Award: Empowered poet 2013- World poetry Canada and Internationals, Vancouver, BC, Canada. Editors choice award 2013- Annodhara Prokashon. Dhaka, Bangladesh.

Web: http://salehmazumder.wordpress.com

Spare Not the Heart's Allure

Do you know what it takes how it feels to breathe

within our magnificence of love?

Time ever sails through soul breaking

into our escape in the flow of unknown destiny.

Soul remains awakened within

the very depths of heart's prayer.

We are raised and beloved in the lover's heart.

Come and open me into my wandering in petals

of folded flowers to live in soft gentle allure.

I will melt in your fragrance that sails me ever on.

We discover love's marvels in a mellowing moon

to ride dreams of mystic haze that always come and muse on our breezes

within. Wind will flourish like a monsoon's drifting rain

and keep falling away in pouring raindrops.

A sudden rush trickles and we are lost inside again.

Do not spare life from any such loveliness.

Rejoice in the heart with warmth of soul's calling

For we are ever so blessed in love's pure clemency.

Annmarie Pearson

Annmarie H. Pearson is a poet, novelist, fiber artist, mother, grandmother and a Reiki/Master Teacher. She resides in New Mexico with her husband of over forty years. She has written two mystery novels, *The Fetish Ruby*, and *A Ruby By Any Other Name: The Stepdaughter*. Also published is a poetry/photograph book, *Nature Rhymes with Natural Impressions,* a collaboration with her husband, William Pearson. www.abpearson.com.

What's It All About?

Awareness is a dangerous thing;
it stirs emotions, opinions
and the dare for one to care.

What's it all about? I've been told
that the world is going to crap. Is this
true or is it propaganda to keep me in fear?

Fear of annihilation as in Uganda;
fear of greed caused by security breaches to
Christmas shoppers;
fear of ethnic hatred or aggravated
homosexuality issues;
fear of children killing children on
school grounds;
fear of global warming and glacier melting
fifty feet per day
due to human hydrocarbons;
or hundreds of fears brought on
by misguided philanthropists.

I watch the news
and observe the nations
of the world. Duck Dynasty
and Dennis Rodman,
celebrities taking issues
into their own hands.

Positive or negative plights is a beginning
of awareness, but individual prayers for
world peace is a more genteel fight.

Oh yes, individual prayers of peace
is definitely needed to join the multi-
millions who hope for a peaceful alliance.
We pray for our world leaders
to adhere to our wishes, too stop the hate,
stop the greed, stop the wars
that are said to be for the sake
—of the citizens' of the world.

The world's citizens want to know,
what's it all about? If not for trade deals,
if not for the rich to get richer,
if not for political power to control;
then why is the world citizens
suffering and dying?
Why are we *no*t being heard?

I am but *one* woman, a mother,
a grandmother, who wants to be heard.
I pray with the multimillions
around the world
for the awareness of peace.

Drezhon Arquis Holloway

Drezhon says, I am like Mandela because we had a movie at school about him and my teacher wanted us to know how good that man was. I love him 1,000 percent because my Mommy told me that he was a great man and he did great things in Africa. I know he was very old when he died, so he could be my play Grandfather. Now he is gone and I feel sad because he was a really important world leader, like Martin Luther King was and he is gone, too. I know I am just a little kid, but kids have to look up to their elders. I am like Mandela because my mommy loves Mandela and my mommy loves me! My mommy said, "Out of the mouth of babes…" but I am not a baby! I will be in 5th grade next year!

Mandela

Mandela wanted everybody to live in love

Not throwing punches, but giving a hug

He threw up his hands in peace

Not to hit with his fists

But to give the whole world a big giant kiss!

Kimberly Burnham PhD

An integrative medicine practitioner, world peace is close to Kimberly Burnham's heart. She specializes in helping improve brain and eyesight health. Published in several Inner Child Press anthologies, including Healing Through Words, Kim won the 2013 SageUSA contest with a poem about her 3000 mile ride across America with Hazon.
http://www.amazon.com/Kimberly-Burnham/e/B0054RZ4A0

Body Talk

Auto immune

cells fighting their neighbors

a multitude of languages

purposes needs misfiring

across the walls

built up

on purpose

are cells willfully

stealing precious resources

taking from the abundance

that lay in a body universe

all around

The selfish gene

drawing in life giving oxygen

red blood cells busy

carrying nutrients to a few

ordering the taking

of precious breaths

for how long will they say

I need all of this

there is not enough

a narrative

swirling in the chaos

molded by demands of life

Looking but not seeing

across a share space

in the beauty of this universe

another individual human system

carbon based life form

cells are talking, laughing even

as each cell takes its needs

the nutrient rich pipelines

flow from head to toe

the difference a few meters will make

As one merges

with the universal needs

of the oneness

who are you

which one

which universe

satisfies your wholeness

today?

Ann White

Ann White is a rabbi, trauma chaplain, and certified grief counselor at a busy Level II trauma center in St. Petersburg, Florida. She is formerly a board certified marital and family attorney and management consultant. She is the founder of Creating Calm Within Chaos and the developer of Stress Rx for Medical Heroes. White is the author of *Living with Spirit Energy, The Sacred Art of Dog Walking – Making the Ordinary Extraordinary,* and *Code Red – a Stress Rx Book for Medical Heroes.* She is a radio host and the founder of the Creating Calm Radio Network. Ann has a passion for rescue dogs – heck, all dogs, and believes dog hair is a fashion accessory.
You can also find her at: www.CreatingCalmWithinChaos.com

Invisible No More

We pass on the road without the blink of an eye

We stand together waiting for the street light to change without the nod of a head

We take the elevator in silence – each in our own world

We ride trains, planes and buses together – strangers

We have become a nation of invisible people

We rush from our home to our car to our office without seeing the clouds in the sky

We are numb to our world – we do not see

We are numb to our lives – we do not feel

Yet all it takes is one moment to change

One moment to smile at a stranger

One moment to hold a door for an elderly man

One moment to open our eyes to the world around us

One moment to open our hearts to another

One moment to feel our connection to all

So open your eyes to wonder

Open your heart to love

Open your mouth to greet another

Open your world to peace

We are one – embrace the possibilities

We are invisible no more

Richard Puckett

I like to write short stories or a poem. If I could be anything in this life, it would be to be a light, for in a light there is no darkness, to give love and forgiveness, to up lift, to build not to destroy, and just to be me.

A Poets Song

A poets song,
deep and not always long,
trails hidden and yet in sight,
love, tears, fears, and joy are in the words spilled,

A poets song,
not meant to be understood at first glance,
deep and steep,
melody and harmony,
bares the soul,
and hides it in one,

A poets song,
Crosses boundaries of race, prejudice,
is about no one and yet about everyone,
is about the wars in the land,
but more often the struggles of the mind,
read, and never understood the same,

A poets song,
is the art of the heart,
the art of the beast with in,
the art of the angel,
it says it all while saying nothing at all,

One such poets songs,
known far and wide,
gifted and wrapped in emotion,
if you know the singer,
then you know something so specail words cannot declare,
such a Poet,
Siddartha, even the name is meant to entice,
the song of life far reaching beyond the imgination,
It is her song she sings, writes, draws, and feeds us humble sheep.

Vicki Acquah

Reading, and having stories read to me at an early age, led to my reciting poetry. I began writing poetry around the age of eight. My Favorite Poet is Paul Lawrence Dunbar. This was a legacy left to me by my grandmother Iona Derrickson.

For The Love Of Mankind

You are not guilty of letting your friends
allow aspartame in our food and drink are you-Not you.?
The room was spinning because
trusted souls allow it in to our drinks and food.

Our undoing -That's not your doing is it ?
No -not you ?Other countries do not
allow this deadly concoction in their
food bulk or soft drink supply.But the
F.D.A is in someones' pocket- Is it yours ?
No not you ?..

Does this deadly poison that many die from quietly
change names and sneak in anyway -
While you grease your palms
and look the other way?
No not you huh? Maybe its
" Sweet an LOW "
on the downlow.
 Did you know? No- not you?

You Say you Love God-well-
I can't tell --So you follow
the culprit that has none.
Because the doctor you
allow to wrack up cash on -
the quick in an out / This places the doubt
on you -Oh Not you- huh ?
Does GMO and Hmo -and the
Cia have a code page
does this destruction of our body functions -
allow you to sleep- tight -at night ?
Yes You !

Do you, toss and turn as
stomachs churn and thyroids burn ?
Does some child born
"Autistic" or worse feel
the wrath of this curse
because of your complacency -
Yes It's you I am speaking to---F.D.A
(MEMBERS OF CONGRESS)
Keepers of the secrets
For the Love of mankind
WILL YOU STOP KILLING US
WITH OUR FOOD?

Kolade Olajumoke

Kolade Olajumoke is an inspirational writer, singer, counselor and with other giftings in her waiting to be discovered. A dynamic lady who believes in hope and dreams of people around her and also offer solutions according to the grace of God upon her. She has featured in a magazine titled 'Lady of influence',written a free poem for her brother's just released poem book and her own book 'Made strong' is well on the way.

THE BEAUTY IN PEACE

Peace, a balm in my soul

Capturing confusion

Throwing it into the sea of forgetfulness

The city longs for you

For your hand of serenity

The people's heart cries out for you

With an unusual desperation

For you, their only place of safety

Peace, your beauty surpasses

Your mission binds all like magnet together

Interwoven in you is the gateway to posterity

Welcome peace, for your absence makes my life

Ebb away.

Gail Weston Shazor

This is a creative promise ~ my pen will speak to and for the world. Enamored with letters and respectful of their power, I have been writing for most of my life. A mother, daughter, sister and grandmother I give what I have been given, greatfilledly.

Author of "An Overstanding of an Imperfect Love" available at Inner Child Press.

www.facebook.com/gailwestonshazor

www.innerchildpress.com/gail-weston-shazor

navypoet1@gmail.com

Daylight Savings

How much does it take to

Turn the hands of angry

Words back to save

Time

Day light, night light

When I was hungry for change

When we whispered about

The coming by moonlight

In quiet loudness

On the skin of drums

Tapping out the slow warning

Even before morse code

And yet my blood memory

Is fading pink

So I reach for a pen

To quickly capture the thoughts

Of my forefathers

Before I can no longer afford

To hear the words

On the winds

And they change quickly

Pushing people from poles to

Medial understandings

And back again until they are gone

Altogether

Buried beneath mortgages and

Loans set about to create

Students and scholars and homes

And cars and businesses and bills

But what about the creation of

Thinkers and healers and griots

And changers and savers

I want to plant a garden

I want to turn back from harvestors

To plowshares

From chemicals to manure

And grasp hands to help me push

Through the soil

Go to bed sweaty from the toil of the day

Forget the GMO's

Let's reforest the rain

Pull the skin back over the coal

My watch can't reset itself to daylight

Saving the sun

My hands will turn it's hands

Because the night is coming

Santos Taino

Writer, Poet, Spoken Word Artist, Author, Creative Artist Hailing from New York, Santos Taino is a seasoned veteran in his chosen craft who delivers a unique perspective and flavor in all of his works.

For more information . . . .

http://facebook.com/santos.t.santiago

FREEDOM AND LIBERTY

Is it the caramel completion that makes you frown Or our biliteracy

Can it be we are too accentous?

Is it presumptuous to believe you find us less then you

I once heard three quarters of a man But that was in reference to Afrikans...but they and we are brothers we share the same Mother

I wonder if I whistle could I be killed I've heard of these kind of injustice ... like Emmett Till

Would I be treated like a king like I mean like Luthor or Martin meaning Trayvon ...Gunned down so I can move on

Can I stand my ground without repercussions

why must me and my brothers be the topic of discussion

I never hear about Canadian immigration

is it my imagination or, Canada doesn't have borders

I've never seen Canadian racial profiling

but I do hear of Mexicans dying Haitians drowning my Africans brothers say I want free

but freedom is never truly free

have we not learned from our ancestry

We still have many walking around blindly

using the N word and pants hanging

Don't you know great Men and Women died for equality

Please pick up your pants and show them some dignity

many died for you and I

many lynched riddled with bullets

beat by whips and bitten by dogs and still many are so blind if they think the cause is over cause we have a black president

don't be fooled we only made a dent

FREEDOM IS NEVER FREE !!!!! I

Urban VooDoo

UrbanVoodoo is a man who has established himself on the National Poetry scene, not only as a prolific artist but also as a host, a radio personality and an activist. Hailing from Inglewood California by way of New Orleans, this spellcaster conjures a strong potion of passion, power and presence with the ingredients that would make for a delicious rue. Call it Gumbo! His flow is a combination of street knowledge and erudition in the tradition of the urban griot. He has performed at the Nouyorican Poets Cafe, in New York; Cafe Istanbul in New Orleans and Strictly for the Listeners in Chicago not to mention all the various stages that he has graced here at home. He is a poets poet a father and a friend, he is City Magic better known as Urban

https://www.facebook.com/uvliveanddirect

BATTLE WEARY

I live carefully

placed At the edge of insanity

Tip Toeing across the front line

Mind constantly questioning our condition My mission....

To liberate my comrads   but most are caught

between Time Warner And Comcast

Blinded by the ignorance Of pop culture

There are soldiers Battle weary and awestruck

Bloody from scars Invisible to naked eyes

Elders act surprised When young folks don't listen...

The truth is,

most recognise that we aborted an unfinished mission,

Bloody and dangerous

 A fetus thrown aside in the second trimester

Liberation has never seen birthing And freedom

is a still born in the hands of a doctor Guilty of malpractice

Who taught the ones who taught my generation?

I hear crickets calling hallelujah In sermons on

Sunday As if they forgot Monday Was when the

liquor store Two doors away opened up For the first time

Confined to concrete Convictions waiting for Jesus

to save only 144,000 from these conditions Even

though millions come to pray

Who wouldn't sell a dream if we all willing to pay? I

am sick of the thoughts that drive us to survival

The cost of living is less stress for those who live

tribal in the bush of Gambian Rainforests Yet we can't

see the forest From the trees

Swear we standing up But we can't seem to tell our feet From our knees

I pray for the day we redeem our ancestors and avenge the fallen

who rather die than stand foot on these shores I am

here only to haunt the seeds of the guilty

Let the shoe rest at the soles Of those who wear

them It's really not my fault that Universal truths scare them...

Diane Sismour has written poetry and fiction for over 35 years in multiple genres. She lives with her husband in eastern Pennsylvania at the foothills of the Blue Mountains. Diane is a member of the Romance Writers of America, the Bethlehem Writer's Group, and the Liberty States Fiction Writers.

Contacts:

www.dianesismour.com
www.dianesismour.blogspot.com
http://facebook.com/dianesismour
http://facebook.com/networkforthearts
Twitter @DianeSismour

the ripple effect

humanity begins
by sticking a toe into rhetoric.
the stir creates a ripple,
in turn causing a wave.
a riptide pummels the identity into submission.
tremulous swells heighten,
blocking the fighting spirit
before society hurls all will against the rough sand
spitting out a shell,
thought ready to conform.

but a spark resides,
an ember awaiting a fan,
to kindle into a flame,
which a gale cannot extinguish.
a fire so hot,
the water steams the next time the toe dips,
leaving a warm current that people follow,
embracing the blaze,
towering as a lighthouse,
beckoning others to venture to the shallows.

droves swamp the shore,
enthralled by the notion
that the light burns brighter than the sun.
caught in the spotlight,
the identity loses sight.
media adds fuel until the land engulfs in fire.
waters churn,
heat swirls the tides,
creating a waterspout,
dowsing the brushfire,
dragging the idiom to sea.

in turmoil,
all hope to remember the paradigm,
the inner strength,
of how one voice can make a difference,
almost dies.
the spark,
which forged others to follow,
wavers.
until looking towards land,
to behold the vision sought.
not one,
but many people,
holding hands to cross the waters,
reaching out to bridge the spark's initiative to
save humanity.

William S. Peters, Sr.

Father, Son, Friend, Writer, Author, Publisher, Radio Talk Show Personality and Producer and so much more.

For more information go to :

www.iamjustbill.com

www.iaminerchild.com

we shall prevail

blood let, blood spilt
upon the woeing plain
life taken, life lost
feel thy mother's pain

battle lost, battle won
the fair cast aside
death claims the anointed
and none may hide

the flowers bloom, die as well
leave naught but shadows behind
dreams abandoned in the quest
for the piper's lute was blind

songs sung, songs of silence
no spirit be thee quelled
upon the plains of woe that day
fifty thousand felled

mothers weep, mothers laughed
for the lot afforded their sons
until the next time the bugle sounds
for no battle is ever won

death stands yet triumphant
and each soul shall it claim
upon the field of battle
it matters not thy name

now daughters, now sons
to those upon death's field
for right prevailed upon each this day
not one would dare to yield

so points made, points are lost
and none forever last
there be no victor when conflict blooms
to fate the die is cast

we shall prevail

Believe in Peace

and we shall have it !

epilogue

a few words from… **hülya n. yilmaz**

Ph.D., Liberal Arts

The 30th anniversary of the founding of the United Nations was marked, among other tributes across the globe, by the Cantata *An die Nachgeborenen, op. 42* Gottfried von Einem had composed to honor the international organization's mission. On the 24th of October 1975, New York hosted the premiere of this opus for which the source was the poem, "An die Nachgeborenen" ("To Those Who Follow Our Wake") by Bertolt Brecht. This three-part poetic construct evidences the author's allusions to the terror-filled Thirty-Years War and World War I. The intensification of the battle forces across Europe in 1939 – the time when the Brechtian verses are known to have surfaced, the looming sufferings of World War II seem transparent to the poet. He thus resorts in this timeless piece to the collected wisdom of humanity and alerts the next generations of readers against silence in face of adversity:

> Truly, I live in dark times!
> An artless word is foolish. A smooth forehead
> Points to insensitivity. He who laughs
> Has not yet received
> The terrible news.
>
> What times are these, in which
> A conversation about trees is almost a crime
> For in doing so we maintain our silence about so much wrongdoing!
> And he who walks quietly across the street,
> Passes out of the reach of his friends
> Who are in danger?

The poem's second part uncovers Brecht's tragic confession, as "[t]he time given to [him] on earth" has passed with him failing to reach the goal for humanity: the spread of knowledge against the infectious mentality behind the war. His verses in the last part, then, assume the tone of a will. The author pleads yet once again with the arriving generations for their retreat from the conflicts of the world, in remembrance of the senseless violence and terror of life the war inflicts on humanity:

You, who shall resurface following the flood
In which we have perished,
Contemplate –
When you speak of our weaknesses,
Also the dark time
That you have escaped.

For we went forth, changing our country more frequently than our shoes
Through the class warfare, despairing
That there was only injustice and no outrage.

And yet we knew:
Even the hatred of squalor
Distorts one's features.
Even anger against injustice
Makes the voice grow hoarse. We
Who wished to lay the foundation for gentleness
Could not ourselves be gentle.

But you, when at last the time comes
That man can aid his fellow man,
Should think upon us
With leniency.

For Brecht, one of the most critically acclaimed world poets of German birth, to offer an autopsy of systematic programs of silencing and mass destructions seems ironic. For, the English word 'war' originates from 'Werran' in the Old High German language ('Werre' in Old English). As for its etymological meaning, the word's outreach capacity disappoints: to confuse or to cause confusion. In its political context, however, it reveals a state of armed conflict; or, as Carl von Clausewitz, the Prussian military analyst defines it, "continuation of politics carried on by other means."

Conflicts carried on by arms – whether in a state of confusion – have been an integral element of world history. Before what became to be the first recorded war between Sumer and Elam in 2700 BCE, tribes had been fighting against one another for thousand of years. The historian, Simon Anglim notes:

> A tribe is a society tracing its origin back to a single ancestor, who may be a real person, a mythical hero, or even a god: they usually view outsiders as dangerous and conflict against them as normal. The possession of permanent territories to

defend or conquer brought the need for large-scale battle in which the losing army would be destroyed, the better to secure the disputed territory. The coming of 'civilization' therefore brought the need for organized bodies of shock troops.

Inherent in the dichotomic 'self' and 'other' relation, therefore prompting fear of a different culture the tribe mentality has been known to often result in war, when a desire to expand was present. With the advancing of technology, war – as can be observed further, spread confusion throughout the ages, indeed reflecting the origins of the word.

While war continues to be a frequent extension of political disputes in the 21ˢᵗ century, as not only stimulated but also justified by the ancient tribe mentality, history of literature throughout time accentuates teachings to the contrary. As early as in the era of the Latin poet Albius Tibullus (ca. 55 BC – 19 BC), humanity's capacity for self-destruction has been questioned and the passionate call for peace has been recorded:

> War is a Crime
> Whoe'er first forged the terror-striking sword,
> His own fierce heart had tempered like its blade.
> What slaughter followed! Ah! what conflict wild!
> What swifter journeys unto darksome death!
>
> Come blessed Peace!
> Come, holding forth thy blade of ripened corn!
> Fill thy large lap with mellow fruits and fair!
>
> *Elegies*, Book I, Number XI

> Who was he, who first forged the fearful sword?
> How iron-willed and truly made of iron he was!
> Then slaughter was created, war was born to men.
> Then a quicker road was opened to dread death.
>
> What madness to summon up dark Death by war!
> It menaces us, and comes secretly on silent feet.
>
> Then come, kindly Peace, hold the wheat-ear in your hand,
> and let your radiant breast pour out fruits before us.
>
> *Elegies*, Book I, Number X

Literary history offers untiring pleas to humanity against the adoption of the tribe mentality and implores world's attention to the anguish of the people during and after the wars preceding our lifespan. Advanced technology with its growingly more destructive products continues to rule over the 21st century. Opposing nations or combating groups within the same national structures are resolved to leave ensuing centuries their violence-conditioned inheritance. Voicing the obvious anew seems to be of vital importance at our times when there still is an audience. "[S]o why do I tell you/anything?" reads the first line in the last stanza of the Adrienne Rich (1929-2012) poem, "What Kind of Times Are These." The poet further composes: "Because you still listen, because in times like these/to have you listen at all, it's necessary/to talk about trees." The intent behind Rich's lyrical work is, as to be expected, not to "talk about trees" but rather, through an imagined common language, to arrive at human love. In the commitment to get to human love – the pivotal subject of any personal or social order, lies the inspirational seed of the *World Healing World Peace 2014, a Poetry Anthology*. The heart and mind behind it can best be told – yet once again – within the framework of literature and its role that is as vital as life itself.

The name of a French dramatist, novelist and essayist is marked as the first writer in Europe to raise his voice against the war: Romain Rolland (1866-1944), the recipient of the Nobel Prize for Literature in 1915. Maxim Gorky (1868-1936), who founded the Socialist Realism literary method, had identified his contemporary within the context of humanism against "the horrors of the slaughter of 1914-1918":

> People say that Romain Rolland is a Don Quixote. To my mind that's the best thing that one can say about anybody. In the great game played by the forces of history with no compassion for us people, a man who craves fairness is also a force, and as such he is capable of opposing the spontaneity of this game. […] In *L'âme enchantée* his heart tells him that soon another, kinder truth the world has long needed will be born. He feels that a new woman will be born to replace the one that is now helping to destroy this world – a woman who understands that she must stimulate culture and therefore she wants to enter the world proudly as its lawful mistress, the mother of men created by her and answerable to her for their acts.

With his conception of the present poetry volumes, Williams S. Peters Sr. justly claims a place in the company of his literary forerunners. For – having created something out of the human spirit that did not exist before, he dedicates to the world of our century a vision that will remain among the most essential bequests of future generations. This modern-day poet of notable accomplishments enunciates the same venerable appeal to the collected wisdom of humanity, as the American writer, William Faulkner (1897-1962) articulated in his acceptance speech for the Nobel Prize in Literature in 1950:

I decline to accept the end of man. It is easy enough to say that man is immortal simply because he will endure: that when the last dingdong of doom has clanged and faded from the last worthless rock hanging tideless in the last red and dying evening, that even then there will still be one more sound: that of his puny inexhaustible voice, still talking. I refuse to accept this. I believe that man will not merely endure: he will prevail. He is immortal, not because he alone among creatures has an inexhaustible voice, but because he has a soul, a spirit capable of compassion and sacrifice and endurance. The poet's, the writer's duty is to write about these things. It is his privilege to help man endure by lifting his heart, by reminding him of the courage and honor and hope and pride and compassion and pity and sacrifice that have been the glory of his past. The poet's voice need not merely be the record of man, it can be one of the props, the pillars to help him endure and prevail.

Whether their lyrical compositions assume an emotion-filled or a neutral tone, the poets who have gathered to contribute to this extensive anthology are kindred spirits with those of whom Faulkner speaks. Their united voice rises through the hope to serve as "one of the props, the pillars to help [humanity] endure and prevail." Their commitment also expands to an invitation for the dissemination of the wisdom behind a warning label that the British poet and critic, Lascelles Abercrombie (1881-1938) left etched in his poem "The Box":

Once upon a time in the land of Hush-a-bye
Around about the wondrous days of yore
They came across a sort of box
Bound up with chains and locked with locks
And labeled, "Kindly Do Not Touch - It's War."

Decree was issued round about
All with a flourish and a shout
And a gaily colored mascot tripping lightly on before
"Don't fiddle with this deadly box
Or break the chains or pick the locks
And please don't ever play about with war."

Well the children understood
Children happen to be good
And they were just as good around the time of yore
They didn't try to pick the locks
Or break into that deadly box
They never tried to play about with war.

Mommies didn't either
Sisters, Aunts, or Grannies neither
Cause' they were quiet and sweet and pretty
In those wondrous days of yore.

Well, very much the same as now
Not the ones to blame somehow
For opening up that deadly box of war.
But someone did
Someone battered in the lid
And spilled the insides out across the floor.

A sort of bouncy bumpy ball
Made up of flags and guns and all
The tears and horror and death
That goes with war.

It bounced right out
And went bashing all about
And bumping into every thing in store.
And what was sad and most unfair
Is that it really didn't seem to care
Much who it bumped or why, or what, or for.

It bumped the children mainly
And I'll tell you this quite plainly
It bumps them everyday
And more and more.
And leaves them dead and burned and dying
Thousands of them sick and crying
Cause' when it bumps it's really very sore.

Now there's a way to stop the ball
It isn't difficult at all
All it takes is wisdom
And I'm absolutely sure
That we could get it back into the box
And bind the chains and lock the locks
But no one seems to want to save the children anymore.

Well, that's the way it all appears
Cause' it's been bouncing round for years and years
In spite of all that wisdom wiz'
Since those wondrous days of yore…
In the time they came upon a box
Bound up with chains and locked with locks
And labeled, "Kindly Do Not Touch - It's War"

In unison, the architect and the contributors of *World Healing World Peace 2014, a Poetry Anthology* join the Greek poet Theocritus (315 BC-260 BC) in his foreseeing love for humanity – the essence of enduring strength to permeate any disruption and decline in any world society:

And may all our towns spoiled by enemy hands
be peopled by their former citizens
again. May they work the fertile fields,
and may countless thousands of sheep fatten
in pastures and go bleating over the plain,
and may cattle coming home in herds
warn the late traveler to hurry
on his way. And may the fallow ground
be plowed at seed-time when the cicada
sings overhead in the treetops, watching
the shepherds in the sun. And may spiders
spin their slender webs over battle-weapons,
and the battle-cry be heard no more.

Idylls: From Number 16

hülya n. yilmaz

~ * ~

Dr. Hulya Yilmaz is a Senior Lecturer at Penn State University. She teaches German, Turkish and Comparative Literature. She is also an available Free Lance Writer, Editor, Literary Translator and Professional Book Reviewer.

for more information, Dr. Yilmaz may be contacted via : hnu1@psu.edu

Dr. hülya yılmaz is a college professor in Liberal Arts with an extensive teaching career. She authored a research book on the influence of ghazal poetry by Rumi and Hafız on 19th and 20th century German literature. Another scholarly work contains her chapter on a controversial novel by Orhan Pamuk, the 2006 recipient of the Nobel Prize for Literature. From her profession, however, she cherishes most the conduct and words of appreciation from a respectable number of students. In her creative work, yılmaz prefers the genres of fictional autobiography, short story and poetry. Presently, she teaches full-time in her fields of specialty; does creative writing; is a self-appointed literary translator and a novice free-lance writer.

Support

World Healing World Peace

www.worldhealingworldpeacepoetry.com

a few words from... Dr. Peter C. Rogers

Clearly, we are living in a time when we are starting to realize that we must work out our own salvation and that no one can do this for us. The road to peace leads to a journey that takes place on the inside which ultimately becomes our physical reality. We are living during a time where God is to be worshipped in spirit. These spiritual times are demanding much more of us in the way of personal introspection. If we are to achieve world peace or peace of any kind, we must first learn to live form our hearts. By living from the heart we will need to be guided by our own personal sense of spirituality and not some old worn out traditions. The spirituality I speak of cannot be taught. To try and teach someone what it is to be spiritual denies the very nature of spirituality because it is unique to each individual. There are many roads to enlightenment and if the road you're on has already been taken, chances are you're on the wrong path.

Each person must find for themselves what it is they have come here for not only in this lifetime but as a conscious being caught up on the wheel of reincarnation and repeated lifecycles. No matter how many times you deny the truth, it's still the truth. Truth is everlasting. There is great freedom in spirituality. Once we are able to shun the age old lies that have been imposed upon us by those living in fear seeking only to control the masses, we will then be able to step out of the darkness and into the marvelous light. This light is the pure essence of God in its entire splendor, God in the truest sense and not diluted by religion or dogma. Once we make the shift from the ideas that have been deeply ingrained in our consciousness by outdated traditions and generations of misinformation, we will have gained liberty from a spiritual tyranny that has long since been imposed upon Humanity. We will begin to seek out the truth for ourselves no longer falling for whatever someone offers us. We will question the status quo and become agitated by things being the way they are. Once this shift occurs, our realities will change and we will finally see the Matrix which is our life for all that it is, nothing more than a mere delusion. Our eyes will be opened and truth will reign supreme because the light of truth will be shed upon falsehood and the dark will no longer be able to exist in the light.

We must each come into our own awareness of peace with each gradual nudge of our spirit. Every occurrence, every lesson and every awakening will slowly beckon us into this full reality. My journey may not be the same as yours but I know for certain that there are many paths and only one summit, I'll meet you there.

Gaia is the planetary consciousness of every living creature that abides on it. It is a Universal phenomenon of creation that took place over billions of years ago. There will never be another Earth and science has yet to find a similar planet that can sustain life. Unfortunately, as a result of countless contributing factors, our planet is dying. We are depleting her in rapid proportions and sooner or later, she will die. When and how soon remains to be seen nevertheless at the rate we're headed, it will most certainly be a premature death. In order to prevent this untimely death, we must all learn to adhere to a higher sense of being. As such we will each need to adhere to a higher sense of being that coincides with elementary and universal truths that support all life.

Peter C. Rogers, D.D., Ph.D.

Dr. Peter C. Rogers, D.D., Ph.D., is a Light-Worker, a Life Coach, Motivational Speaker, Minister of Metaphysics and Spiritual Counselor.

He is the author of ***Ultimate Truth : Book I***, ***Universal Truth: Thinking Outside the Box : Book II*** and the up and coming ***One Hundred Disciplines to Higher Consciousness*** : ***A Conclusive Synopsis on Spiritual Principles***.

Dr. Rogers is a skilled lecturer and teacher of the Master Key System. He teaches an extensive class and has appeared on several shows to present this ancient system of manifestation formulated by Charles F. Haanel over 100 years ago. In 2010, Dr. Rogers founded a spiritual counseling practice called **TRUTH Dynamics** to help assist people in their quest for self realization.

Currently, he serves as the president of a Non-Profit organization called P.E.L.S.A which he and his wife formed in 2006 to assist people in overcoming addiction.

Dr. Rogers has been a student of Spirituality and Metaphysics for the past 20 years and in 2009, he received a Doctorate of Divinity in Spiritual Counseling as well as a Doctorate of Philosophy in Metaphysics from The University of Metaphysical Sciences. He currently resides in Long Beach, California where he continues to devote his time and energy writing, lecturing and mentoring others on their spiritual journey towards higher consciousness.

Peace
Quotes

We, Veteran's for Peace, view peace as a positively active and creative process which requires courage, commitment, endurance, vigilance, and integrity. Peace is a struggle toward unity, and it is characterized by an absence of violence in all its forms, including discrimination based on gender, age, race, religion, social and economic status, ethnicity, and sexual orientation. Those who labor for peace are called peacemakers because they tirelessly pursue nonviolent solutions, work for economic and social justice, celebrate diversity, and strive to build relationships between adversaries through education, conflict mediation, and humanitarian relief. We recognize that peace is both a means and end simultaneously, and that it is never finally or fully achieved. This is because change and growth require some degree of tension or conflict. Historically, such conflict has provided the impetus for military solutions. Thus we, Veteran's for Peace, strongly believe that the greatest obstacle to peace is militarism with its reliance on violence and war. We further believe that peacekeeping action should only be accomplished by a legitimate international body.

Committee to Define Peace, Veterans for Peace

You can't separate peace from freedom because no one can be at peace unless he has his freedom

Malcolm X

Peace is always beautiful.

Walt Whitman

Since wars begin in the minds of men, it is in the minds of men that the defenses of peace must be constructed.

UNESCO Constitution

Time itself becomes subordinate to war. If only we could celebrate peace as our various ancestors celebrated war; if only we could glorify peace as those before us, thirsting for adventure, glorified war; if only our sages and scholars together could resolve to infuse peace with the same energy and inspiration that others have put into war.

Why is war such an easy option? Why does peace remain such an elusive goal? We know statesmen skilled at waging war, but where are those dedicated enough to humanity to find a way to avoid war. Every nation has its prestigious military academies - or so few of them - that reach not only the virtues of peace but also the art of attaining it. I mean attaining and protecting it by means other than weapons, the tools of war. Why are we surprised whenever war recedes and yields to peace?

Elie Wiesel

If we have no peace, it is because we have forgotten that we belong to each other.

All works of love are works of peace.
I was once asked why I don't participate in anti-war demonstrations. I said that I will never do that, but as soon as you have a pro-peace rally, I'll be there.

Mother Theresa

The word *liberal* comes from the word *free*. We must cherish and honor the word *free* or it will cease to apply to us.
It isn't enough to talk about peace. One must believe in it. And it isn't enough to believe in it. One must work at it.

Elenor Roosevelt

World Healing ~ World Peace
Tee Shirts & Baseball Caps
Now Available

just $ 20.00 each
www.worldhealingworldpeacepoetry.com

all proceeds used to distribute Books to the United Nations & U.S. Congress

just $ 40.00 each
www.worldhealingworldpeacepoetry.com

all proceeds used to distribute Books to the United Nations & U.S. Congress

just $ 20.00 each
www.worldhealingworldpeacepoetry.com

all proceeds used to distribute Books to the United Nations & U.S. Congress

just $ 25.00 each

all proceeds used to distribute Books to the United Nations & U.S. Congress

other significant Anthologies from . . .

inner child press, ltd.

www.innerchildpress.com

World Healing World Peace

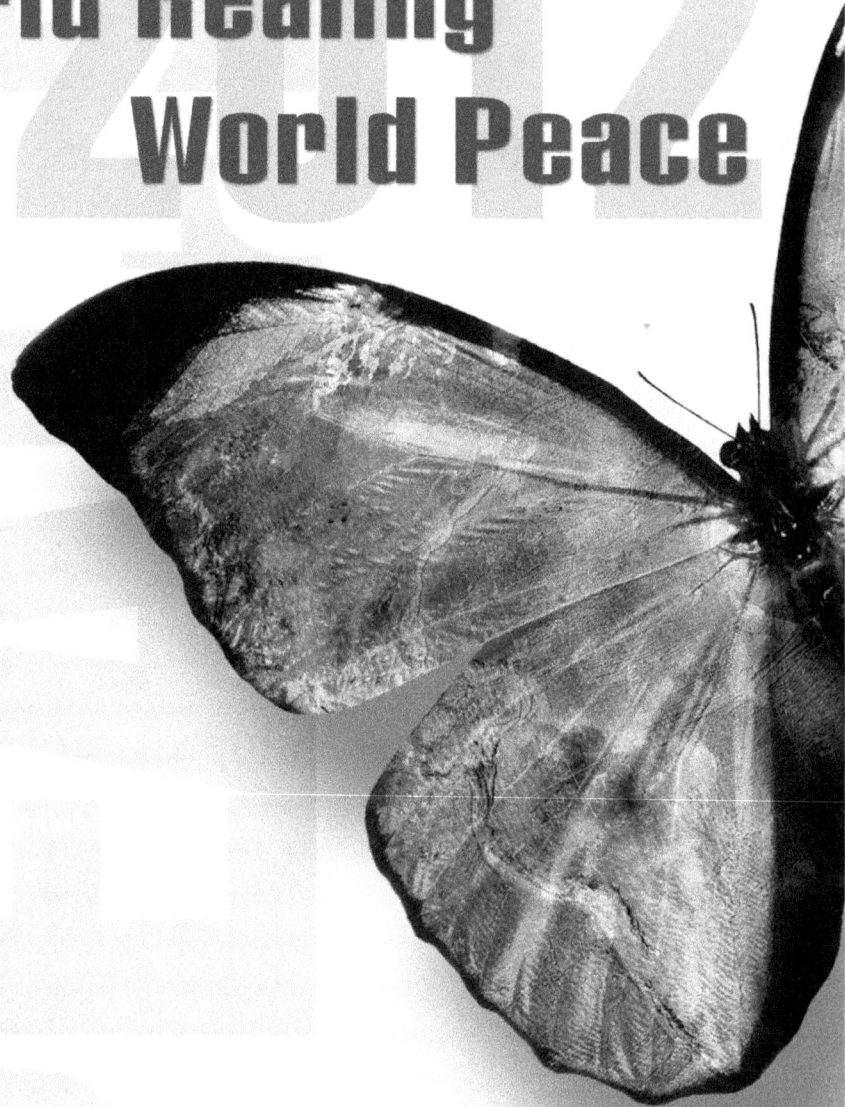

2012

A POETRY ANTHOLOGY
Volume 1

2012

World Healing
World Peace

A POETRY ANTHOLOGY
Volume 2

Mandela

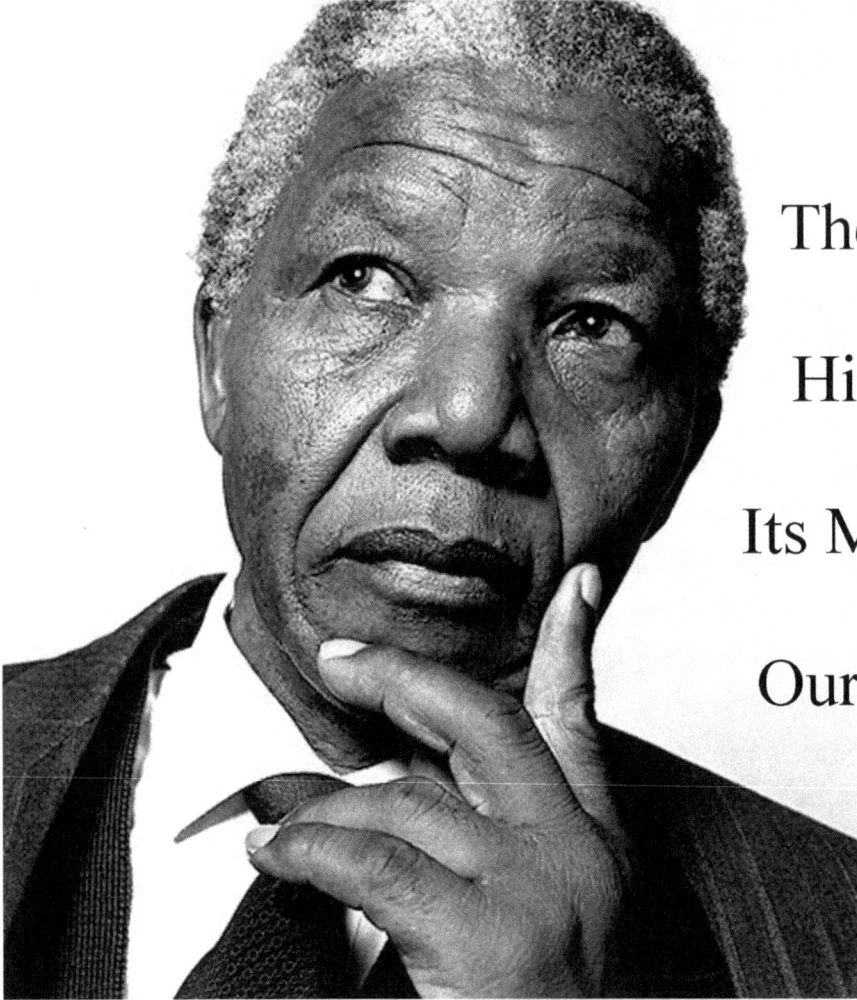

The Man

His Life

Its Meaning

Our Words

Poetry . . . Commentary & Stories
The Anthological Writers

A GATHERING OF WORDS

POETRY & COMMENTARY
FOR
TRAYVON MARTIN

healing through words

Poetry ... Prose ... Prayer ... Stories

142

PEOPLE OF EXTRAORDINARY TALENT

P.O.E.T.

ANTHOLOGY

FINDING YOUR VOICE
CLOSED MICS
DON'T GET FED

VOLUME 1

PEOPLE OF EXTRAORDINARY TALENT

P.O.E.T.®

ANTHOLOGY

FINDING YOUR PURPOSE

A.C.T.I.O.N.®

Artist
Coming
Together
In
Outstanding
Numbers

SPEAKS LOUDER THAN WORDS

VOLUME II

i

want my

PoEtRy

to . . .

a collection of the Voices of Many inspired by …

Monte Smith

a collection of the Voices of Many inspired by . . .

Monte Smith

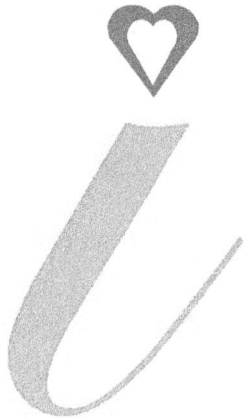 i

want my

PoEtRy

to . . .

volume II

PuZzled

...when the PIECES don't seem to fit.

Poets & Writers for Autism Awareness and Acceptance

Inner Child Press

Inner Child Press is a Publishing Company Founded and Operated by Writers. Our personal publishing experiences provides us an intimate understanding of the sometimes daunting challenges Writers, New and Seasoned may face in the Business of Publishing and Marketing their Creative "Written Work".

For more Information

Inner Child Press

www.innerchildpress.com

intouch@innerchildpress.com

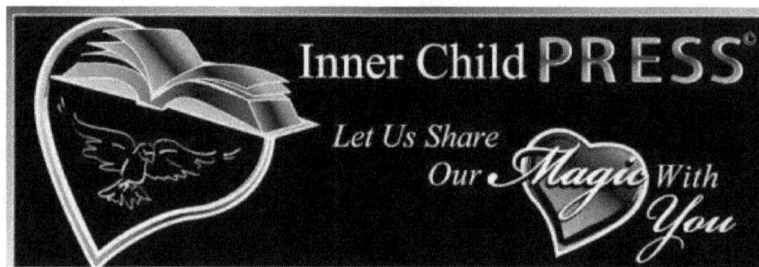

www.ingramcontent.com/pod-product-compliance
Lightning Source LLC
Chambersburg PA
CBHW081229090426
42738CB00016B/3238